REBUILT THROUGH RECOVERY

The Good, The Bad, The Ugly of Recovery Stories

By
Anthony McCauley

Co-authored by Seven Amazing World Changers

2021

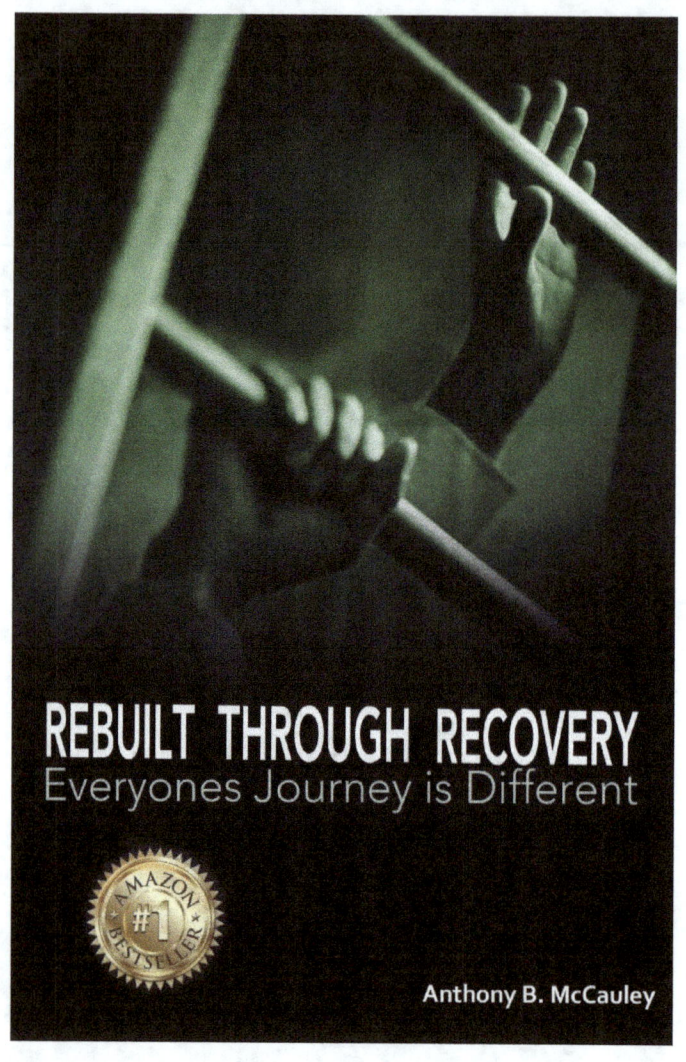

Copyright © 2022 by Anthony McCauley

All rights reserved. This book or any portion thereof may not be reproduced or used in any manner whatsoever without the express written permission of the publisher except for the use of brief quotations in a book review or scholarly journal.

First Printing: 2022

ISBN: 979-8-9860894-1-6

Ordering Information:

Special discounts are available on quantity purchases by corporations, associations, educators, and others. For details, contact the publisher at the above-listed address.

U.S. trade bookstores and wholesalers:
Please contact info@businessofbooksmastermind.com

DEDICATION

This book is dedicated to the sick, suffering, and the families who have lost loved ones to the disease of addiction. We pray this book will show you the experience, strength, and hope to deal with your situation, or provide you with an opportunity to get this book into the hands of someone who needs help. We send love to our families, and all those who support "Rebuilt Through Recovery."

ACKNOWLEDGEMENTS

I would like to express my gratitude to my fellow authors in this book. You have followed through with me on this journey, and you believed in me with this vision and collaboration. All of you have amazing stories and you are miracles. Thank you for your tremendous understanding of this idea. The best is yet to come! #RISEUP

Anthony B. McCauley

PREFACE

The goal of this book is to share real-life stories of those who have overcome the obsession to use and abuse substances. The book features six authors who have poured out their stories in the hopes that you will change your mind and get the help you need. Learn from these lessons and apply their experiences. We want this book to get into the hands of the right person who will share their testimony of how they overcame a life of addictive behaviors.

TABLE OF CONTENTS

DEDICATION iv

ACKNOWLEDGEMENTS v

PREFACE vi

LIST OF AUTHORS IN CHAPTER ORDER 1

BEAUTY FROM ASHES 2

IT'S NEVER TOO LATE 17

DESPERATION TO RESTORATION 33

HOW MY FATHER SAVED MY LIFE—TWENTY-FOUR YEARS AFTER HE DIED 46

ONE MORE DAY 59

THE GOOD, THE BAD, AND THE UGLY OF MY RECOVERY STORY 74

HOW LOUD IS YOUR PAIN? 89

REMEMBERING CORDA 107

ABOUT THE LEAD AUTHOR 108

LIST OF AUTHORS IN CHAPTER ORDER

1. Megan Price
2. Anthony Bernard McCauley
3. Chase Campbell
4. Garry A. Carlson
5. Derrick L. Pearson
6. Gloria Mildred Douglass
7. Hoss Tabrizi

BEAUTY FROM ASHES
Megan Price

Behold the candy-coated, sugar plum, tidied-up version of the disaster that is my past, and how I got to where I am today. My goal in putting this colorful story into black and white is to illustrate how I was able to turn my pain into beauty through the love of Christ. It is a journey through the timeline of my life from the earliest point I can remember until now. While there were good times, they seemed to end up as bad times more often than not.

Like Alice chasing the white rabbit, I spent the first forty years of my life sliding down dark tunnels until I finally hit rock bottom; then, I kept sliding and fell two floors lower into rock bottom Hell. Who knew Hell was so complex? It truly has so many levels. Believe me, when I tell you it is true, I was there dancing with the devil, constantly wrestling demons and barely clinging to life. I was an empty shell of myself with no feelings or emotions. I was completely detached from my soul, living through a constant out-of-body experience. I truly did not care if I lived or died, so I dare to say, I was suicidal. As I flew through life like a kamikaze, I was definitely on autopilot.

I know this all sounds very macabre and indeed it was, but hang in there with me, and you will see how this phoenix rises from her ashes. I hope that my story will serve as a light in someone else's dark tunnels and that my testimony will become an inspiration to those who are dwelling in their wilderness as I once was. My prayer is that someone out there will be able to relate to my triumph over addiction and that it will ignite an awakening deep within their soul.

I was born in a suburb just outside of Cleveland, Ohio called Brunswick. I have one sister and two brothers; we never needed anything growing up because my father was a wonderful provider. However, I remember my parents were always fighting, which led to the most traumatic moments of my early childhood. When I was six years old my parents divorced, so my mother decided to move us to Florida to be close to my grandparents. This resulted in splitting our family in half.

My younger brother and I went to Florida with my mother while my older siblings stayed in Ohio with my father. We landed in beautiful Palm Harbor in 1983 with all the beautiful people who lived beautiful lives—at least it appeared that way. Looking back now, I see how plastic my existence truly was. It was the era of "Keeping up with the Jones," devoid of any real substance and emotional value.

When I realized that my dad and siblings were not coming with us, sadness began to dim the light of my spirit. This trauma was the beginning of a long path of mental health and substance abuse issues. It was most certainly the source of my depression and drugging. It took me countless therapy sessions and about thirty years to figure out that this trauma was the root cause of my sadness and anger. But, we will talk about my thirties later.

At seventeen, I was diagnosed with clinical depression and anorexia. My condition only worsened as I got older. I was never comfortable, never happy, and never satisfied. You could give me the world, and it still would not have been enough.

I hated school. Though I enjoyed academics, the politics, fakeness, and popularity contests never sat well with me. I started attending a private high school with an advanced curriculum where the classroom setting was one-on-one, so there was no drama. I graduated high school in 1994. Because I was so eager to flee the nest, this graduation date was one and a half years earlier than usual. I wanted nothing to do with high school kids. Although I did have a best friend; she and I were seventeen going on twenty-five.

Her older sister was dating a big-name DJ in Tampa, so that had its perks. It was a crowd far removed from the high school circus. My best friend and I became club kids. We were getting into twenty-one and up rave clubs with VIP status when we were barely old enough to drive. Being a club kid in Florida in the '90s was equivalent to being a fixture at Studio 54 in the '70s or '80s. All we did was look good and party, and we loved every minute of it. We were essentially living like rock stars, and that is exactly how we partied. Alas, what goes up must come down. Remember that.

I have always been very independent, so I could not wait to be out on my own, free from rules and regulations. I was never one to conform. I eventually ended up moving to Tampa when I was nineteen. It was easier than making the forty-five-minute trip across the bridge every time I wanted to party, which I was doing regularly. Looking back, I truly know that it was God who helped me make it into my forties without any consequences for impaired driving.

Throughout this crazy lifestyle, believe it or not, I managed to maintain my innocence. My bestie and I were very coveted and protected by the crowd of older friends that we were with. We had a lot of "big brothers," most of who were bouncers, that looked after us. I was also attending college during this time and kept a 3.2 GPA. My grades were good even though I picked up a few extracurricular habits along the way.

South Tampa is a very upscale, posh area filled with yuppies. Everyone is always dressed to the nines like they just popped out of a Rick Ross video. There is no shortage of money in that city. It was a very high-maintenance lifestyle with fast cars and fancy nightclubs.

Before I knew it, life had gone by so quickly that I failed to realize that I was developing a major drug problem. What used to be just for fun was turning into a steady lifestyle. A typical night in the town would always involve a bottle of wine, at least, and what we called powder, (cocaine). It was the norm to have a little toot on the dance floor and, of course, there was no shortage of the number one club drug in the '90s—Ecstasy. Being so close to Miami, I could get my hands on anything I wanted at any time, which is a perk of being young and attractive I suppose.

Sprinkle in some horrible relationships, a couple of failed marriages, and lots of hangovers, and you can have a pretty good idea of my twenties and early thirties. I was a functioning addict, so I could hold down a good job, one of which was a liquor representative for one of the largest distributors in Florida. I represented the Moet Hennessey portfolio, so when I tell you I was living in a music video, I'm not lying! That job was nothing shy of training me to become a better alcoholic. We would have business meetings that consisted of wine and liquor sampling on Friday mornings at 9 am. After we sampled and learned our products, we would have to run our daily sales route. It made for an interesting day, to say the least, but I learned how to keep my composure and my tolerance.

I completed my Bachelor's Degree from St. Leo University and purchased a house by the time I turned thirty. Unfortunately, being Miss Independent only landed me drunk and alone. I had the house, the job, and the car, but I was still not satisfied. I was chasing something but I didn't know what or why, so I tried to fill the void with a side hustle that ultimately ended up being my demise.

I was already a liquor rep so I decided to add "Street Pharmaceutical Rep" to my resume. I ended up getting married to the man who at the time was my "partner." We were slinging pills together, so naturally, I married him. At the time, he was the closest thing to stability I could latch on to, so I did.

During this time, pill mills were popping up all over Florida. I was living in Pasco County at this point, the epicenter for prescription drug abuse, human trafficking, and methamphetamine. This was a far cry from the lifestyle I had led in Tampa, and the bar lowered significantly. Now in my early thirties, drug addiction was starting to take its toll. The idea that I had any control of my life, I now know, was just an illusion. I ended up addicted, for the first time physically, to oxycodone.

I battled my pill habit for over three years. I was detoxing myself with suboxone and methamphetamine, just to make it to my next pill refill once a month, maybe more if you knew the right shady doctor. It was a vicious cycle. My monthly prescription consisted of three hundred 30 mg oxy, sixty Somas, one hundred and twenty Xanax, and one hundred and twenty 10 mg methadone. It was enough to kill an elephant.

It's safe to say my marriage ended after only one year, but no big surprise there. When you live a Godless life, nothing lasts. Then, one day, I got a phone call from my high school sweetheart. He had just got out of prison from doing a fifteen-year bid. He was my knight in shining armor, or so I thought. He whisked me away to North Carolina where I thought I was going to finally have a normal life. I truly thought that a man had the power to magically transform my existence, or at least I hoped so. Society taught me that this was the way to be happy.

He played right into my delusion, promising to take care of me and swearing that he would not allow me to fall back into pills. I had been looking for a savior for a long time, and I made the mistake of thinking that he was the one who could do it. We ended up having a son, and, of course, the drug use continued into this relationship as well. Adding a child to the mix of this toxic mess was a recipe for disaster. This relationship could best be described as oil and water. It became extremely volatile, so I will spare the gory details.

The pain and suffering I endured, both self-inflicted and otherwise, spun me into more intense levels of addiction. The drugs mixed with a slew of fresh mental health issues including post-traumatic stress disorder postpartum depression, and trauma-induced anxiety. These struggles were driving me over the edge.

I lost my job as a Territory Manager, (outside sales) when I got in a car accident that totaled my brand-new car. I wasn't even the one driving. I put every penny I had into getting that car so that I would have a safe ride for my newborn son. At this point, I was broke, so I couldn't afford another car.

The vehicle flipped upside down into a ditch where it crumbled up like a tin can. When the car settled, I found myself in the back seat on the roof getting punched in the arm by a side airbag. Again, looking back, I know it was by the grace of God that I walked away from that wreck without a scratch.

That was the first night I can remember encountering and receiving directions from an angel. Right before the crash, the voice told me how to position myself upon impact, and it worked. Had I remained in the front passenger seat, I would have been decapitated because the windshield came down into that area like a serrated knife. As I was flipping into the back of the car, I was being scraped down the fronts of my arms by the jagged glass.

Adding insult to injury, not only did I lose my transportation and my job, but my relationship with my son's father ended as well, leaving me homeless. I had no choice but to seek refuge in a domestic violence shelter while I could formulate my next plan of action. This was a very difficult time because I was terrified to leave my room, let alone leave the house.

My anxiety made it difficult for me to go out and look for work or engage in social settings. Because I was once a professional social butterfly, I was not stripped of my self-efficacy. Though I found it very difficult to think for myself anymore, I could remember what it was like to be independent.

I had completely lost my identity. Since I had no friends in North Carolina and I barely spoke to my family, I was alone. How did this all happen? I was so controlled that I didn't even realize I was being controlled.

The few people that I did know outside of work weren't the kind of people you would want to meet in a dark alley. I would have hardly called them friends, yet they were the only people I had. Looking back, I can't help but think that this was by design.

Needless to say, I was completely alone. I didn't want to leave my room because I feared being drugged, kidnapped, or worse, given a "Hot Shot" (a mixture of lethal drugs given to someone with the intent to kill them). Living in constant fear, I couldn't go to sleep because I was afraid of waking up in a different place. So, I started using amphetamines to stay awake. The uppers only accelerated my paranoia, making things far worse. Lack of sleep was causing me to lose touch with reality.

At this time, I began receiving direct attacks from the devil. I have zero doubt that it was him and not some half-witted demon. This was not a battle. It was a full-blown war.

Not knowing how to escape, I was engaging in heavy spiritual warfare. I dwelled in that wilderness for about eight years until I finally reconnected with the angel that whispered instructions into my ear during my accident. This time it wasn't just instructions; the angel gave me a battle strategy. But, let's not jump ahead.

My mother came to visit me from Florida and immediately began making plans to get me as far away from North Carolina as possible. I ended up moving back to Florida with her and my stepfather. I was attempting the get myself together so I could be a better mother.

Leaving with my mom required me to leave my son in the care of his grandparents because I couldn't take him out of North Carolina. There were custody barriers, so this was the only option I had. However, I knew that this was the safest option for my son until I could get things straightened out.

The reality of the situation was also that I was not fit to raise my son at that time. I lost everything—no house, no car—and I wound up back on drugs. Being away from my son only made my condition and my drug abuse worse. I was running in circles trying to numb the pain because it was the only thing I knew how to do. Instead of fighting harder, I sat in my depression and became fair game for the devil. He had me in the palm of his hands now more than ever.

I still loved my son's father—you might even say that I worshiped him—so imagine the agony I was in. He betrayed me. On top of that, I was now three states away from my son. I felt like a failure, and the pain of the breakup just iced my cake.

I was going stark raving mad with sadness which turned to anger that was fueled by vengeance and revenge. By this time, child services became involved. Luckily, we didn't lose custody even though our lives were in shambles. His parents got temporary custody at our request. It was by the grace of God because truth be told, my son's father was no more fit to raise him than I was.

As I continued to spiral out of control, I ended up getting arrested for a misdemeanor drug charge. It seemed like things were steadily catching up to me. I had finally hit rock bottom, or so I thought.

After spending thirty days in jail, my parents bailed me out and sent me to rehab in Boca Raton, Florida. I was an official patient at Lighthouse Recovery Institute, conveniently located near Mara Lago, Donald Trump's prestigious resort. I stayed inpatient at Light House Recovery for four months. Upon my completion of the program, I hesitantly decided to go into sober living where I proceeded to stay for the next three years.

Things were looking up, and the custody issues with my son started to smooth over. We agreed on joint, fifty-fifty custody even though I am convinced we still wanted to kill each other at that point. It was what was right for our boy. Our son needs his mommy and his daddy, so I'm glad that we were able to be mature enough the realize this and to do what was best for him. When it comes to Mason, we maintain a healthy balance. Our differences always take the back seat. This is the one thing I can say we do right is raise Mason. Even though sometimes the choice was hard and it hurt, we always made sure that he was safe and sound.

My son came to spend some weekends with me in Florida and, eventually, he lived there with me for a year. Fortunately, my father agreed to take care of me as long as I was working on my recovery, which gave me the opportunity to get back on my feet and care for my son. To this day, I am grateful that I never had to resort to creative alternatives, like prostitution, to survive. I know many who were not as fortunate, and I watched that lifestyle kill them inside. The streets of Pasco County are cruel and make it almost impossible to stay clean. I was fortunate to not have been on that path.

Sober living was quite an experience, I bounced in and out a few times, thinking that I had it under control only to realize I was not and never would be in control. It is true that once you become complacent you are the most vulnerable.

While I was living at the DaVinci Recovery Home in Pasco County, there were many ups and downs. Among the cycle of relapses and getting kicked out, I found myself sitting in a jail cell once more. I managed to total my car again, which was the last possession I had in the world. This time the accident was my fault.

I fell asleep at the wheel (living out of your car with PTSD makes for many sleepless nights) and crashed. This was the aftermath of getting kicked out of sober living for relapsing. I was out there for about a week.

A chain-link fence caught my car, acting as a safety net that kept me from colliding with a brick wall at 50 mph. I am blessed that God kept the path clear, so I didn't hurt anyone. He even decided to spare me as undeserving as I was.

I was charged with a misdemeanor DUI, and got one of the lowest possible bail amounts. However, this time, nobody came to bail me out. I had burned all of my bridges; my family was angry with me, I didn't have any real friends left, and I was truly alone. I thought I'd hit rock bottom before, but that was just the tip of the iceberg. This time, I sank like the Titanic.

It was amid the chaos that I remember praying to the Lord asking him to release me from the Hell that I was in. My angel gave me some ammunition, and I was using it. I finally had enough of the high cost of low living, and I was ready to take a new approach. This was the first time I called on God and asked him to help me with conviction and repentance. Wouldn't you know, I ended up getting out of jail five days before my arraignment, which never happens.

I was so excited to be out of jail until reality set in and I realized that I still had nowhere to go. I had no ride, no money, and my phone was dead. The only place that I could go that was safe and drug-free was back to DaVinci, where I would have to eat a lot of crow.

I was fortunate enough to hitch a ride with a man who was at the jail to visit his son. Although I had previously broken the rules and gotten kicked out, Angie, the owner of DaVinci Recovery Home, decided to take me back. This time, something was different. I truly think she could tell that I had the ultimate intervention.

Throughout my journey, I religiously attended recovery meetings, but this time there was a new element. Even though I constantly worked through AA and NA programs, once I got out of rehab, I continued to relapse. I would stay sober for six or eight months until, boom, I returned to using. Why was I doing this? The program was helpful, but I think that the twelve steps only introduced me to the ultimate enhancement of my life: my spiritual awakening.

I met God in the Echo Pod of the Pasco County Jail. A cell block area doesn't seem like a very holy place, but it goes to show you that God will go anywhere for His children. It was in this place that I began seeking the Lord, I mean truly seeking the Lord, and He came swiftly to my rescue. This was the beginning of the biggest transformation of my life. It turns out that Jesus was the missing element this whole time. The solution was right in front of my face, all I had to do was ask.

My point is that even though working on myself in AA and NA proved to be efficient, the steps were only the path that brought me to the answer: God, the Father. I think that twelve-step programs are designed to bring us closer to Jesus. Through him, we experience the ultimate healing and transformation.

Once I began walking with Jesus, my entire life changed; the way I talked, the things I wore, and the people I surrounded myself with all began to align with my renewed lifestyle. He picked me up, and He cleaned me off. As I continue to transform into my highest self, the blessings abundantly manifest. He has broken the chains of addiction off of me for good. My cravings for drugs and alcohol are gone. He broke me out of the toxic cycle of living that I was in, bouncing from halfway houses to relapsing every six months.

Because of Jesus, I finally made it back to North Carolina with my son, where I have been able to celebrate his last two birthdays without having to hop on a plane. I have a house, a car, and a couple of businesses—all of the things that I went without for years while I was in the wilderness. Through Him, I am confident enough to use my voice. Now, I even started to sing for the praise and worship team at my church. After being silent for so long, God has given me the courage to speak out. The pain that I endured has transformed into beauty, which I can use to inspire myself and others.

I am now an advocate speaking out against drug abuse, domestic violence, and human trafficking. My personal experience, strength, and hope come from the power of the Almighty. There is no denying that fact. I recently became a certified North Carolina Peer Support Specialist and a CCAR Recovery Coach. I'm also in school at St. Leo University working towards a master's in clinical social work and psychotherapy.

My transformation has catapulted me into another dimension where I am walking faithfully and confidently into the future because of the One who left the ninety-nine white sheep just to save a train-wrecked black sheep like me. Not trying to sound too preachy here, but I hope you can see that, if He did this for me, He will do it for you too.

It took me forty-four years to finally figure out what my heartstrings feel like. It is amazing how God has aligned me with the right people in the right places at the right times, and He continues to do so. These people have helped me to move closer to the Lord and to understand the transition that I have endured. I have been blessed to see God through both prophets and apostles alike, each of whom carried our God-ordained messages. Angels come in many shapes and sizes, and it is a blessing when you get to meet them face to face.

Although my life looks like a series of unfortunate events, I can say that I do not regret my mistakes or the many wrong paths that I chose. The fact of the matter remains. Without those experiences, it would be impossible for me to fully understand and develop the calling of God in my life.

It is from these experiences that I have formed the capability and understanding to help others out of their dark tunnels. It has been through my newly formed relationships that I have begun to formulate a clear understanding of what I needed while I was down and out. I understand and have the ammunition needed to go back onto the battlefield and bring more souls out of the war.

I look at all the time I spent with the devil, how he would taunt and torment me to the point where I thought I was losing my mind. Toward the end of my drug use, I spent a few times in the psych ward, which is truly the devil's playground. I played mind Olympics with Satan and his crew of demons twenty-four hours a day, seven days a week.

I made it through all of that so that I could be strong enough for someone else who isn't. As a soldier, I help to pull the wounded off the battlefield and equip them with tools, the very tools that I needed when I was the one with one foot in the grave. I now understand that I am special and that not everyone has the same gifts and capabilities that I possess. Not everyone has what it takes to step back into battle, and not only do I continue to come out, but I come out with brothers and sisters in tow. My gifts are not any better than others—we all have different callings that are all equally important—but God chose me for this.

I want to help people like me figure out how to become who God has called them to be. I am in the Special Ops of God's Army, and I am not afraid to go into the darkest depths of Hell, look the devil square in the eyes, and smile as I gracefully pull souls out of his grip by leading them to Jesus. Being protected by the armor of God assures me that I will be safe. If there's one thing that I am certain of, it's that I can stand on the word of God. I am fulfilled, and I am blessed. I am beyond grateful for all of my past, but I am even more grateful for my eternal future.

Like a light in the darkness, I strive to let people know that the solution is out there waiting. What kept me going during my recovery was having a sponsor, attending meetings, and taking accountability. In the beginning, I was just going through the motions, but being in the rooms of AA and NA helped me survive until I found the ultimate solution in Jesus.

Jesus is the One who has truly taught me how to live my best life. I am also grateful for all of the amazing friendships that I developed along the way. While I was in the muck, I couldn't see that the brothers and sisters beside me were my friends. The devil had me think that everyone was my enemy.

Now that I have matured spiritually, I realize that the strongest friendships are the ones forged in battle. I guess what I am trying to illustrate here is that we are at war and we need to start looking at one another as fellow soldiers instead of enemies. The more we fight each other, the more the devil wins. This information is all in the Bible. If you don't already know, the answers are all laid out for you. The entire battle plan equipped with ammo is right at your fingertips.

As I continue to transform, I realize that serving others is what He has called me to. We keep what we have by giving it away, paying it forward, staying humble, and remaining grateful always. Continue to be of service in any way that you can. If you see an opportunity to help someone, then do it. If you have an opportunity to compliment someone, do it; you may be saving their life! We are all fighting through our struggles, and just because it looks good on the outside doesn't mean that the inside isn't caving in. Next time you see a stranger, smile at them and watch the spark that you ignite.

Today I live to watch Him turn graves into gardens. I know for certain that Jesus made beauty from my ashes when he pulled me from the embers. No one is too far from God's reach. He reached down into Hell and snatched me right out of the devil's hand. I will spend every last bit of my breath telling my testimony of how Jesus pulled my dry bones from the grave.

I was created for a purpose, and that purpose is to tell you about Him so that you can live the life He intended for you. I am a shining example of God's handy work. From a half-dead junkie to a supermom who's running two businesses and getting her master's degree, we do recover!

ABOUT THE AUTHOR:

Megan Price was born in Cleveland, Ohio, and raised in Palm Harbor, Florida. She is a single mother to one child, a boy named Mason.

She is the founder and CEO of Divine Calling LLC, a Christian-based call center platform, which provides roadside assistance. Megan is a North Carolina Certified Peer Support Specialist and a CCAR Recovery Coach. She is a life-long mentor that uses her experience, strength, and hope to help others, specifically women, recover from traumatic events.

She completed her bachelor's degree in business administration, graduating with honors from Saint Leo University in 2006. She has returned to her alma mater where she is currently pursuing her master's degree in clinical social work and psychotherapy. Upon completion, she plans to pursue her LCSW and begin a private practice focusing on trauma and substance abuse therapy for both veterans and civilians.

She has a passion for psychology, social work, and recovery education. She is active in volunteering for causes such as the Stand Up for Cancer Telethon and dedicates her time to the Salvation Army. Megan is also very active at her church, True Life Ministries in Wagram, North Carolina, where she volunteers and sings on the praise and worship team. She also provides peer support and motivation by leading a recovery ministry in her community.

Ms. Megan Price works with women and youth who are victims of domestic abuse, human trafficking, and drug abuse. She helps survivors transition back into their communities upon recovering from traumatic events. She helps the victims to regain their independence and go on to lead prosperous lives. Megan also provides women with ongoing mentor support.

Ms. Megan Price uses the success from her life experience, battle with addiction, and trauma to help other women regain their confidence and independence. She strives to be a light in the darkness for anyone in need.

IT'S NEVER TOO LATE
Anthony McCauley

"It's never too late to become what you could have been."
- *Author, Anthony McCauley*

Life is full of experiences, but it's often difficult to come to this realization. I had to learn that the things we face come from our own decisions; these are the consequences of our actions, whether good or bad. The setbacks of life position us to endure and bounce back to change our situations. I have endured a lot of setbacks that I have learned from. At times, I made the same mistakes over and over, taking life for granted and justifying it with my own stupid notion that I am having fun. And I did have fun, but sin is designed to make you feel that way. However, hang in there with me!

My story is not to glorify my past sins or tell war stories about my past lifestyle. I found myself indulging so much in crack cocaine that the consequences led to a rock bottom. I fell prey to the rituals of getting high. I did not choose this way of life, and I have no idea why this is my testimony. My spirit says that it's not about me, it's about that still suffering addict or alcoholic that needs to hear about my experience and strength so that they can build up a sense of hope. Sharing my testimony also helps me to stay sober and to keep the life that I have built for myself.

The setbacks that come with living as an addict are fruitless, vain, and downright futile! If you think for one moment that you can find happiness in crack cocaine, or whatever your drug of choice may be, then you are in for a cold and ruthless ride. You don't even need a ticket to ride; there are no weight and height requirements, no socio-economic class. Substance use has no face. My prayer is that this book will reach the right people, whether they are ready or not so that they can hear relatable testimonies of recovery.

My aggressive ranting as I tried to rationalize my addiction cut me off from emotional expression. This left me justifying my own ill-nature and denying I had a problem. I soon found myself in this state of **D.E.N.I.A.L.** (**D**on't **E**ven k**N**ow **I A**m **L**ying), and it left me feeling scornful! I ended up like a fierce tornado, destroying everything in my path: spending money when I should've been providing for my family, paying a drug dealer's mortgage before paying my own, and keeping Anheuser Busch stock prices above average with my excessive drinking.

I had totally lost control. Anything that causes problems and health risks are something that needs fixing. When I found myself in this state of mind I had to realign and rearrange my thought process.

Please don't get me wrong, when I was drinking and smoking dope, I felt invincible. It was as the drugs and liquor transformed me into Super Anthony! This way of thinking caused me to be the life of every party, a people-pleaser, and an attention-seeker.

It got to the point where I was unable to limit the amount of what I was consuming, so I started to develop a higher tolerance. Because of this, I needed more to feel the same effect, which led to lots of blackouts and ending up in strange places. I have survived two overdoses!

I grew up in a loving blue-collar family. My father, Bernard McCauley, was a disciplinarian. He had rules that he enforced with consequences if we broke them. My dad is no longer in my life, but I think of him every day. I know that he would be proud of me. My mother, Mary McCauley, is still with us, and it is such a blessing to have her in my life. She supports me in all I set out to do! I love speaking with her, and she knows everything about me.

I was a talented athlete and excelled in football, basketball, and track throughout high school. I had every expectation of receiving a scholarship to a good college, one that would provide me with an education that my parents could not afford. I successfully balanced school and sports as I achieved goals in the classroom and on the field. This led me to play three varsity sports, which took my popularity right to the top!

I wasn't a straight-A student, but I maintained decent grades knowing that, if I performed poorly, my father would address the issue. Anytime I received a grade of C or below, my father would let me know that I needed to pull my grades up or I would have to stop playing sports.

There is one person that deserves accolades for my development and transition during high school: Coach Donnie Holt. He saw something in me and encouraged me to improve myself as an athlete. Sometimes, I questioned his approach to coaching and teaching, but I knew that he had my best interest at heart.

Coach Holt was a very intelligent man, and he knew the game well. He had already achieved successes in sports and academics, so he knew what it took for the next generation. I had the luxury of being around him often because he lived in my neighborhood. He cared so much for all the students, regardless of whether they were athletes or not. I learned a lot of fundamentals under his coaching like the ethics of practicing and the basics of exercise.

I graduated high school in 1983. My class elected me as the "most friendly." I thought this was cool to be the friendliest person in the class, and I carried myself that way.

This background information is just a foundation to let you know that I started life in a position to excel. The choices I made after I graduated from high school are no reflection of my upbringing. My behavior as I grew into adulthood was not the result of anything planted inside me during my adolescence.

I remember my first encounter with alcohol and marijuana. During my senior year, I suffered from a bad knee injury that derailed my dreams. No college or university even looked at me after that, so I developed deep-seated feelings of resentment. Directionless at the age of seventeen, I sought a way to fill the void and discovered drugs.

In the 1980s, a drug epidemic of crack cocaine swept through black communities. During that time, the response was not oriented towards the public's health. Instead, the focus was entirely on criminalizing addiction by passing laws to lock up drug users with excessive prison sentences, such as mandatory minimums. Despite widespread accounts that link crack cocaine to inner-city decay, little systematic research has analyzed how the emergence of crack affected urban crime.

The abuse of substances escalated in my life. My drinking evolved to become excessive. After anything that happened in my life, it was an occasion to drink. When I started using cocaine, I was just flirting with the idea of snorting powdered cocaine, but it became the beginning of turmoil. It was so dressed up to make you feel good, and you could party forever without sleep! I do recall times when that inner voice was tugging at me, letting me know that I was wrong for putting chemicals inside my body. This voice wasn't a side-effect of drug use, it was God covering me and speaking to me, even through the darkness.

I would always find myself in situations that would require me to bully my way out of. In one situation, I found myself indebted to a drug dealer who would normally allow me to pay him later. Well, I could not pay him back on time like I normally would because I was already in the hole with several other dealers around the city. So, the dealer was very angry with me, and he wanted his money immediately.

He pulled a gun on me and pointed it at my head. When he forced me onto my knees, I thought that my life was going to end tragically by getting shot in the head by a drug dealer. What a hell of a way to go! My life flashed before me, but I didn't hear any shots.

This immediately put me in defense mode. I grabbed the gun, taking the risk of getting shot. I actually overpowered him and took the gun. Soon, I had him on the floor in the same position that he had me in. I was shaking and in tears; my heart was pounding so hard that felt like I would have a heart attack. I just knew that my heart was going to explode.

Out of nowhere, I heard the voice of God say, "I will never leave you nor forsake you!"

This calmed me down. I gave the dealer his gun back and told him to never do that to me again. I was in a fit of rage, and defense mode. I overpowered him, with my size and stature—I had him shook, as he never saw this side of me before. He was quite shaken at the moment because he knew I had the upper hand. The dealer knew the gun wasn't loaded, this was all a game that he thought was funny because he had the drugs, and I wanted what he had! To prevent any bad blood between us, he handed me a large amount of cocaine and told me to go on my way.

I know it sounds foolish, but I found myself in a situation to die that day over two hundred dollars worth of drugs. Having to constantly deal with the emotional turmoil that resulted from the feeling that I had ruined my life made a mess of everything.

It left me wondering, "How can I come back from this? How do I deal with these setbacks? How can I reshape my mindset as it's dwindling?"

Don't get me wrong, I had plenty of solid days where I felt stable and had moments of clarity. I convinced myself that I could maintain this lifestyle in moderation instead of having to walk away from it completely.

I have always tried to lead a godly life. Even when I felt like a dead man walking, I didn't care what anyone thought of me. I was smart enough to know that it was no power of my own that was guiding me in dark places. My own power is not what brought me back from two overdoses; it was the power of prayer. Those who have experienced a similar path know that the struggle through darkness is led by a demon. Still, I wouldn't listen to the people who believed in me.

At this point, I began to pray to God saying, "What is it that I need to change?"

I immediately got my answer. The only thing that needed to change was everything.

I want anyone who is reading this book to know that, when you put mood-altering chemicals into your body, you ruin the balance that God has equipped us with. When I was struggling, I had no idea that addiction is a medical condition. Using cocaine even once makes you crave it for as long as you live. If you don't take the necessary steps and recognize that you are powerless over it, you will get caught in a vicious cycle until you hit a rock bottom that leads to jail time, institutionalization, and death. The abuse of cocaine has psychological, emotional, mental, and spiritual consequences.

After years of using powdered cocaine, I found a way to turn that obsession into something stronger. Another way to ingest it is to add baking soda and water and then heat it up. This is how you create a monster called crack cocaine! It's called crack because, once you put it on a pipe and light it, it crackles for a second. Then, the vapor from it sends your mind into a readiness that you never knew existed.

This drug makes you lose all respect for yourself and those close to you, and it sucks up all your money. I thought I could outsmart crack by using my suave knowledge to smoke it in moderation. By doing this, I thought that I could still achieve the elements that make up a decent life—a wife, children, a house, and a good job. Boy, who was I fooling? I was so disillusioned by the belief that I can be the man that everyone thinks is so cool, the man that everyone looks forward to seeing. Well, keep reading I got my butt handed to me!

I discovered crack cocaine during the drug epidemic in the 1980s. It was the thing to do. Even though the epidemic hit forty years ago, I think it's worse off now. Drug use is still kicking butt and taking names, breaking up families, and pushing people to rock bottom. While in active addiction, I was able to stay clean for significant periods of time. I became the employee of the month, found a wife, and successfully raised children.

Even though I was doing great, that sleeping giant was just watching and waiting for me to hit a breaking point. More setbacks were coming. My addiction proved me wrong for thinking that I could use drugs in moderation. Every time I started using again, I set myself back a little further.

I found myself in places that I knew I had no business going to. I felt as though I always came up against a blank wall and didn't know which way to turn for help. I had exhausted everyone with my sinful nature of so-called "having fun."

One time, when I traveled to another state, I remember looking around and thinking, "Surely there aren't any drugs in this place."

Of course, I knew better than that, but I was just trying to convince myself that it was the start of a new path. I thought that I could escape the setbacks.

This little town was so full of what I wanted that I trapped myself in situations that reflected my old habits. Eventually, I was stuck in the middle of a major drug bust. Amid the police and DEA agents sorting out people in the dope house, an officer came up to me.

He pulled me aside and asked, "Who are you?"

Here I was, freshly shaven and good-looking. The officer begins to tell me that this house was under surveillance for months, and he asked me how I ended up there. I let him know that I was on a break and that I asked someone if they knew how I could find a good time with cocaine. In other words, I talked to a junkie-looking person on the street to see if they knew where I could get some crack.

Even at rock bottom, I never forgot about the spiritual life that I had walked away from. The grace of God was always covering me so that, someday, I could share my story. I'm a living example of how setbacks are nothing more than opportunities to come back stronger. It's possible to be clean and sober if you remove anything that doesn't line up with being a productive member of society.

The officer proceeded to pull me out of the house and said, "I don't know who you are, but I need you to walk away from here. If I see you look back, I will come and arrest you."

So, what did I do? I cut a trail so fast and got the heck out of there, only to hear the ones who were being arrested say, "I told you he was a cop!"

How quickly they seemed to forget that no one cared about who I was when I walked in with a pocket full of money. It didn't matter who I was, cop or not; they gave me the royal treatment at that crack house! And, just to clarify, I am not a policeman.

As I walked away from almost getting busted, I had the same old classic lines that so many of us addicts have, "God, I promise I will not do that again."

Who was I fooling? Not God!

Any chance of turning to my family was out of the question. They were sick of hearing the same thing from me without seeing any changes being made.

Without my family to depend on, I called on the name of Jesus every time I got into trouble. I learned quickly that character is developed by the daily discipline of responsibility, but I had lost all sense of prayer in my life, except for when I needed Him to bail me out. How did I get here?

Well, this was just one episode of many from the early stages of my using and experimenting. Remember that anyone—your colleague, boss, or most successful friend who looks like they have it all together—could fall to the temptation of drug use. Addiction has no face! It will set you back to the level of hitting rock bottom in your life.

How could I suppress this empty feeling and the sadness of my life slipping away? At the end of a not-so-great day, I found myself saying, "To hell with it!"

As I started to use more frequently, my tolerance increased. I'm telling you, do not flirt with this drug. If you are ever around it, don't just turn and run, I urge you to flee! I'm not only talking about crack or cocaine. I can only speak about my drug of choice, but still, I urge you to never give in to the temptation of using any kind of drug. Drug use will only result in setback after setback. It causes a dwindling effect that you will later look upon only to realize that you've lost your mind and all the things that you have built up.

Cocaine causes the neurons in your brain to release an abnormal amount of dopamine, which is already produced naturally. When you consume any mood-altering chemical, cocaine in particular, it prevents the normal recycling of chemicals in your brain. This sudden burst of dopamine is what provides the user with the feeling of euphoria. According to the National Institute on Drug Abuse (NIDA), dopamine is a transmitter that's present in regions of the brain that regulate movement, emotion, motivation, and feelings of pleasure. The rush of dopamine strongly reinforces the behavior of drug use. This is what kept me repeating the same vicious cycle.

As an addict, I was accustomed to having my dopamine levels ten times above the natural amount. The reward of ingesting a hit of crack motivated me to do it again and again and again and again, times a million! I think you get the idea. Please let me inform you that, eventually, this kind of drug use causes problems. I remember realizing how the drug was affecting my health when I could see my heart beating through my shirt as if it was coming out of my chest. I even had two overdoses.

Seeing how my health was deteriorating, I was thinking, "This is it! Something is not right."

But my addicted mind spoke louder and said, "What are you talking about? Man up!"

As I reflect on my setbacks, I can never forget the things that I did to hurt those closest to me as well as myself. The obsession to keep using kept me thinking about my next move to continue getting high. When it came to drugs, I would kick into mastermind mode and manipulation—what was next, who could I befriend, or what dealer could do some trading—for me to get what I needed.

There were so many times that I found myself in a dark place where I had no business being. There are so many stories that I can share with you about this lifestyle of drug abuse. I know firsthand what it's like to lose everything, get it all back, then lose it all over again. This is called insanity—doing the same thing repeatedly and expecting a different result. Life does not work that way.

I had to admit that I was powerless over drugs and alcohol and that my life had become unmanageable. I had to come to terms with the fact that I had hit an all-time low: rock bottom.

I often asked myself, "How can I even try and fool myself into thinking that good things will happen for me?"

In my mind, I knew that God cared for me and would provide for me. Still, I couldn't get past the fact that my body craved mood-altering chemicals. How could I force myself to never touch the drug again? How could I eliminate the notion that moderation would suffice? How could I become truthful with myself and those closest to me?

Endurance, steadfastness, tenacity—these were just a few of the ingredients that I needed to move forward with cleaning my life up. My attitude had to change from this nasty selfishness to humbleness, appreciation, and gratitude. After all the years of masking, hiding, and falling behind, there had to be a rude awakening to help me prepare for better things to come.

I needed someone to tell me that morning was coming instead of the sorrowful dark night that I expected. I wanted so badly to believe that all of the struggles that I had faced were just the cost of cultivating a better life ahead. No matter what you have lost and no matter what things flood your mind with doom and gloom, you can't move on to a life of peace until the core issue is resolved.

Even in the darkness of my life, I felt the spirit of God tugging at me. You see my friends, God did not move; I moved. So, to get my life back on track, I moved my focus back to God and repented.

Even when I was on the wrong path, even when I was up against the wall, even when the only money that I had was from manipulating others, the spirit of God was still with me. As my desire for sobriety grew, the enemy within me was punching back as it tried to hold on to the life of addiction.

I remember sitting alone in a hotel room with plenty of drugs to last until I blacked out. During those times, I was so lonely that I would read the Bible that the hotel kept in the little drawer of the dresser. With tears flowing down my face, I would ask God to keep me safe when I used the drugs.

I pray that this doesn't sound crazy to you, but I refuse to sugarcoat these events from my life. To describe the setbacks that I have endured, I need to remove my mask so that I can be transparent. Everything you're reading comes from actual situations that happened during the blindless that I experienced during my active phase of addiction. I am dedicated to keeping it real with anyone who reads this book.

You must believe that God's grace exists in all of our lives. Personally, I never questioned God's presence. I always knew he was with me, even during the fear, worry, and disconnection that comes with addiction. I maintained my sense of awareness and trust in God, knowing that I could turn to Him when I had no one else.

Keeping my faith in God, I reached a point of complete surrender. I knew that He would give me the strength to overcome addiction so that I could reach a state of peace. I always told myself that one day I would express myself with a sober mind and present myself with clean hands. I knew that I could bring strength and hope to a broken world.

You can make use of your sufferings and mistakes regardless of what has happened to you. The only question is, what are you going to do with your life? Are you going to choose life? Or are you going to choose death?

My regular drug use was a ritual that used up a lot of my energy. All I had to do was shift that energy from getting to doing something positive instead.

I must tell you that I have been in rehabilitation centers throughout my active addiction days. I entered a treatment facility in Florida and started a program that changed my life! The facility,

Stepping Stone, was in Jacksonville. This humbling experience changed my life and gave me the tools that I needed to get back on track.

From the first moment of my arrival, I was nervous, but I wanted so badly to get clean. At Stepping Stone, I received a binder full of information and a progress-based treatment plan. I also conducted some research, reading articles that seemed like a piece of gold in my hands!

For the first time on this whole roller coaster ride of addictive behaviors, I was willing to accept the structure of my treatment plan. The goal was progression. After day fifteen, I advanced to another level and moved on to the "step-up" treatment. This is where the rubber meets the road.

When I moved to the next level, I would hear other patients call Stepping Stone "the North" because you get more freedom. To make it there, the staff needs to verify that I was stable enough. The counseling became more intense as I got into the core issue that landed me in rehab.

The structure was great. I was on my own, but they gave me a schedule that I had to comply with. It was all designed to regain a sense of normalcy in my life. By this time, I was beginning to look and feel a little bit better. My health was improving, and I gained some weight. I even started exercising, journaling, and reading. I was so happy to be in the facility because I knew that I was right where I needed to be at that moment.

I met some of the most wonderful people, both staff and residents, that had the same issues as I had. Many of us keep in touch to this day. I had a counselor named Juan D who took my sense of reality for a ride. This man was the most straightforward and in-your-face counselor. He let me know that he was not there to be my friend, but instead, to help me get better and to figure out coping skills for after I left treatment. Once I reached this level of stability, my time at Stepping Stones would be over.

Juan D assured me that, if I listened to him and followed his treatment plan, I would be able to identify some issues that I have never dealt with before. This scared me at first.

In my mind, I was thinking, "Here we go again with this."

First, I had to respect this man because he was a professional. I gave him respect based on the fact that he was willing to help me. He was stubborn, so I wasn't able to alter his approach or question his knowledge. He was just like me.

Juan D showed me how group settings worked within the facility. Group sessions are a time of learning and opening. It was important to understand that there was a certain level of confidentiality in the facility. You shouldn't share another patient's stories with anyone else. I doubted whether I would make it through treatment with Juan D, but I devoted myself to discovering where my obsession with drug use comes from.

Once I became accustomed to the schedule, I was willing to do anything to make the necessary change in my life. No matter what, I didn't want to go back to rock bottom. My spirit focused solely on transformation. I became a great resource for those around me, but I had to remember that I was no better than anyone else. We all had the same story.

The group I was in ended up becoming a tight-knit community. We had respect and love for each other, which made for a great atmosphere. In bonding, I learned that some people are sicker than others, so they need more time to heal completely.

During this time, a national study group called the "Life Onions" approached me to participate in one of their projects. This group focuses on peeling back the layers of the onion to help discover your reason for relapsing. A counselor named Patty M ran the program, and I came to respect her. At first, I thought that her approach seemed unhinged. The tools that she used would have me laughing, crying, yelling, or talking it out. The outcome was usually very amazing.

I will never forget one activity that allowed me to have a reflective experience. She put a handheld mirror in front of my face and told me to talk to the person I saw. After having this mirror experience, my life has not been the same!

The time I spent in Jacksonville was the best thing that could ever happen to me. It changed my life! I left there what an attitude of gratitude, and I felt motivated to experience this new life. I closed the door on the struggles from my past. I had identified that the core issue of all my failures came from a fear of success. You see, I had no problem accomplishing things, I just didn't know what to do once I reached the plateaus of success. This is why I sabotaged every opportunity that came my way.

I left the facility with the necessary tools to cope with this fear of success. Would I FEAR (**F**orget **E**verything **a**nd **R**un), or do I FEAR (**F**orget **E**verything **a**nd **R**ise)? I chose to forget everything and rise above it all.

The way that I bounced back proves that I am a miracle. I have always believed in God and will continually include this in any of my writings going forward. My spiritual life remains focused on an awareness of God's presence in my life. This is how I continue down the path of sobriety.

I must be led in all things by my awareness of God and trust Him in all I do. Just having this awareness always brings a sense of tranquility to me. The fact that I hit a rock bottom in my life dealing with addictive behavior allows me to freely share with you that faith is the messenger that carried my prayers to God. I encourage those that are dealing with similar issues to pray to God with a sincere heart. Have faith and trust that He hears your cry, even during darkness.

When you hit rock bottom and you're sick of being sick, when you no longer want to deal with setbacks, you can then begin to truly experience the inner consciousness of God. You may have already experienced it. It will become necessary for all the distractions to be removed so that your personal relationships and the mending of your heart will begin to overcome those old habits. It's never too late to become what you could have been!

I pray that my testimony will get into the right hands. Whether it be you or one of your loved ones that need to hear our message, these real-life stories show that addictive behaviors are beatable. Come to an understanding and have an awareness that life is full of strain and difficulties. Your situation can change when you decide to remove the negative, thus releasing some of your personal baggage.

I'M NOT ANYTHING, AND YET I AM EVERYTHING! IN MYSELF I AM NOTHING, AND IN CHRIST JESUS I AM EVERYTHING I NEED TO BE!
-Author Anthony B. McCauley

ABOUT THE AUTHOR:

Please see the Lead Author's full biography at end of the book.

DESPERATION TO RESTORATION
Chase Campbell

This is a story of how I went from hopeless to hopeful, which I am sharing with the hope of inspiring hope. If you are struggling with addiction from whatever it is, I would like you to know that I have been there. I was actively using drugs and alcohol for about one-third of my life. I started experimenting with substances at seventeen and continued until I was twenty-seven. It wasn't bad at first, but it ended horribly.

Ten years later, I remember looking back and thinking, "How did I get here?"

I was in a deep hole of darkness. I never thought I would make it out, yet here I am. Although, it wasn't by my own doing that got me out of it. It was by the grace of God and the people who came before me that found a solution and passed it on. I am truly grateful to say today that I am no longer a part of the problem; I am part of the solution. So, I would like to share my experience, strength, and hope. I am going to tell you what it was like, what happened, and what life is like today in a general way.

Just to give you an idea of where I come from, I grew up in a small town in North Carolina called Rockingham. At some point, it was a decent place to live with a lot of plants and mills for different industries and a booming economy. We also had a NASCAR track that attracted tourists. However, for as long as I can remember most of that was gone. There is a lot of poverty, crime, drug use, and not many things to do. I don't blame any of my life and my decisions on where I am from, yet for a while, I was a product of my environment.

I believe strongly in the disease of addiction, better known by the CDC as substance use disorder. I know for a fact that I suffer from the illness, yet it doesn't define me today. I also believe that it can be passed through genetics, but it doesn't have to be. It could skip generations or occur over long-term drug use, your brain chemistry can change and be the first in your family to have the disease.

I think I inherited it from both my mother and father, although they were never part of my life. My mom passed away from cancer when I was twelve months old. She could have gotten chemo when she was pregnant with me, but if she did, I wouldn't be here today.

My mom suffered from this disease, but I don't think her disease had progressed as much as mine. I say that because, when I was at my lowest, I would put my addiction and myself above anybody and anything. No matter who or what it was! My mom made the ultimate sacrifice so I could live, and I am grateful for that today.

As far as my father, he was a great man from what I hear, just sick like myself. He was never really there. He stayed on the streets, drank forty ounces, and would say he was coming to see me but never did. Because I wanted the family everyone else had, I resented him as a child. I didn't know why he chose alcohol over me, but I did know he was an alcoholic. Even when I was too young to understand what that meant, I still knew that I never wanted to be like him.

I had a lot of self-pity and resentment growing up for the cards I was dealt in life, but I never let anyone know that. I bottled it all inside because I didn't want to seem weak or less than. I was never okay, but I didn't want you to know that.

My father's mother raised me, and she did the best she could. My granny was the best woman I ever met! She was somewhat of an angel, my best friend, my mother, and my father. I grew up in a middle-class home. I never went without anything. I didn't always get what I wanted, but I always got what I needed.

My granny raised me with morals. She always took me to church, but there was always some sort of disconnect. I believed what I heard in the church because my Granny and other people at church weren't faking their feelings. I just didn't understand why I couldn't connect on that level. Maybe deep down, I blamed God for my parents not being there. When I would pray for answers, I felt like I didn't get any.

Now I believe that all of my experiences and feelings made me who I am today. What I know is that God always has a plan, but we only get a glimpse of it. There was no abuse as a child or any trauma, yet I always felt less than my peers because I didn't have a traditional family. Alcohol and drugs were never in the household, but I saw them from a third person's perspective.

Several of my family members were on drugs. I won't get into the details, but let's just say they would borrow things without asking and it would end up at the pawnshop.

I would ask my granny, "If they love me, why would they do that?"

She would just say, "They are on drugs Chase."

I didn't know what drugs were, but I knew I never wanted to do them. Red Ribbon Week and DARE class had me convinced that only bad people did drugs. In retrospect, it is very ironic. Most of the things I said I'd never do are exactly what consumed me. At some point, I convinced myself that all of my childhood teachings about drugs and alcohol were wrong. I justified in my head that it won't be that bad if I just try them because I didn't think I would get hooked.

Eventually, in high school, I was at a party where I smoked some weed and drank. I was with friends who were good people, so I didn't think the weed and alcohol could be so bad. I will say that I loved the feeling the substances gave me. They made me feel euphoric, happy, and just like everyone else. These are all of the things that I ever wanted to be.

I never imagined where drugs would take me. When I first graduated high school, I wasn't experiencing any consequences of my drug use. At that point, I didn't let alcohol or drugs change me. It was just recreational. I had a choice whether I used it or not. It wasn't controlling me because I didn't get hooked initially. With or without it, I would be okay.

Nevertheless, the disease is progressive, so it always gets worse. I went to college in western Carolina in the mountains and then things started taking off. I had goals of getting a degree in business administration. Not long after I started college, I got involved in other things that seemed more important than my education.

To make a little extra money, I started selling illegal drugs. I felt important because everyone wanted to be my friend and hang out. I would say I got addicted to the lifestyle and everything that came along with it. First, it was just profit, then it became doing what I wanted to do for free, then it became very unmanageable. I got involved in pharmaceuticals and things took off.

Profits increased but my addiction did as well. It went from a habit to an addiction. I needed the medicine to function. I knew it wasn't good for me, but I didn't want to stop what I was doing, and I wasn't aware that I couldn't stop if I tried at the time.

Eventually, consequences started to kick in and things started to spiral. I started having seizures and started losing things. First, I totaled my car. Then, I got dropped from school. Finally, I had to move back home with my granny.

She didn't understand what was going on with me, but she knew something was different. I left home as an optimistic youth and came back as the shell of a man, hollow on the inside. My granny had gotten sick, and it seemed like the more her disease got worse, so did mine.

I would love to tell you that I was the best grandson I could be, but unfortunately, that was not the case. You would think that after all my Granny did for me, I would do all I could for her, but this disease I have makes me think I have to put addiction in front of everything else. It centers in my brain so all my thoughts come from it, and at this point, getting high was all I could think about.

The worst part is that I couldn't even enjoy it anymore because I was more concerned about what I would do when I ran out. It's like a voice in your head that never stops. You chase a feeling that you will never achieve again, yet you will go to great lengths by any means necessary to get that feeling.

Eventually, my granny passed away, and my addiction took off even more. The guilt of not taking care of my granny was weighing hard on me, so all I want to do was numb myself at all times. All of my other family was no longer dealing with me because they knew that, if they got close, I would hurt them like I did everyone else. Looking back, I really cannot blame them. They were just protecting themselves.

Without my granny, I felt alone in the world. All I had was me and the addiction. Unfortunately, it wouldn't leave my side. I would go from couch to couch just to avoid living on the streets like my father. I had plenty of friends at first, but eventually, I burned so many bridges that I had nowhere to go, all with the mentality of a victim. I would meet women and use them until they had to wash their hands as well.

I never had a problem working and getting a job because I had a strong work ethic and was good at talking to people, especially in job interviews. When you have a strong addiction, you will do whatever you have to do to fund your habit, so I didn't mind working. My real problem would be keeping the job. Employers aren't exactly thrilled about someone coming to work high or dope sick either.

I remember getting paid and telling myself that I would not spend this check on drugs, but I lied. I could maybe convince myself that I would just get one of whatever drug I was using at that time. Once I got one in my body, I had a compulsion to use it as much as I could.

At this point, I was not picky about what substances I used, just anything to change the way I felt inside. Any drug was acceptable to me. A lot of things I said I would never do were the usual. The abnormal had become the norm. The things that I had previously judged others for doing became second nature to me. Nothing could stop me except maybe going to the ATM to withdraw money and having insufficient funds or my dealer running out.

I would put my addiction over basically any human necessity—food, sleep, anything. At my lowest, I remember going into a dollar general and stealing food just so that I would have something to eat. I also had food stamps and money in my pocket, but I already had plans of how I was going to spend both to get the next fix.

Essentially, I could not afford to spend anything that didn't involve getting high. I would rather risk getting caught or being hungry than having to stay sober. That is the disease at its finest. Your brain gets rewired to think that the next high is more important than anything.

I remember at different times people would ask me, "Why don't you just quit?"

Deep down I knew that I couldn't stop, nor did I want to, but pride and ego would never admit that. I would often get defensive because my disease wanted to protect itself.

In my head, drugs were the only coping mechanism I had to live life, so the thought of not having them horrified me. Over time, life got worse and worse as a result of the way I was living. I wasn't even living though. I was just trapped in a miserable existence. I stayed in a homeless shelter for a bit until they wouldn't even let me stay there. Then I was really at rock bottom. I had hit plenty of sufficient bottoms before that, yet it was never enough pain to stop. I still had resources until they were all gone.

I felt like drugs were my best friend that never left my side, until eventually, they didn't do what they used to do. There was no happiness or release, it was just survival because I didn't know how to live life without them.

One night, I took a lot of different substances and went into a blackout, I don't remember anything except what I was told. I woke up to my girlfriend at the time furious and kicking me out. Somehow that night I lost my phone and all of my money. At this point, I had nothing to my name except for a couple of trash bags full of clothes.

When I tried to go to the homeless shelter again, the preacher there asked me if I could pass a drug test. I couldn't, so he wouldn't let me stay. He told me that I needed to get help. I took that very personally because I was asking for his help, and he is telling me to go get help. The truth is, him not helping me is the best help I could have ever gotten.

At rock bottom, I went to a storage container that I knew I could stay in and no one would mess with me. It was April 2019, and it seemed like the coldest I had ever felt. It was extremely dark because there were not any windows or anything like that, so no light could come in. I also felt alone, I didn't have my phone to contact anyone. Even if I did, I probably didn't have anyone to call. I am sharing this because the way I felt on the outside is the same way I felt on the inside—cold, dark, and alone. I hope I never forget those feelings because I never want to feel that way again.

While staying in the storage container, I finally had a moment of clarity! At that moment, I believe God allowed me to see myself as I was. I was where I was because addiction took me there, and I willingly went. I started thinking about what that preacher said about getting help, and I sincerely prayed to God to help me. Whatever help there was, I wanted it!

In a position of surrender, that moment changed the whole trajectory of my life. Life beat me into a state of reason where I was willing to put in the action to change my behavior. It wasn't long until God started answering my prayers. Doors started opening, and all I had to do was be willing to walk through them.

Over the next sixty days, I started gaining hope. People began walking into my life that had been through the same or similar situations. I would meet people at meetings that suffered from the same disease I suffered from, yet they were happy and had good lives. That gave me hope. I went to detox at a place called the safe house, and I also went to an inpatient treatment center called Samaritan Colony. These places saved my life. I am forever grateful for the people I met and for the things they taught me.

Detox got me well enough to deal with the withdrawal. The safehouse introduced me to recovery, and the colony gave me tools on how to live in recovery and stay sober. I heard a lot of cliché sayings that were so simple yet so complex and seemed profound to me at the time such as, "nothing changes if nothing changes" or, "if you always do what you have always done, you will always get what you have always got."

I knew that what I had been doing did not work in my favor, so I was eager to do something different. It's been a few years since then, and my life has drastically improved. I utilized the tools I was given, and I continue using them today. God will move mountains, but He may give you a shovel.

I found sobriety by using the twelve steps and by developing a real relationship with God through prayer and meditation. My whole life, I tried to use different substances, money, women, and whatever else to fill this hole in my soul. It never worked; it only made it bigger. The only thing that can fill that hole is God and the purpose he has given me. I believe that my purpose is to help others find a way out of rock bottom. I won't say early recovery is easy because it's not, but the reward far exceeds the work. Nothing that comes easy is worth having and nothing worth having comes easy.

I love my life today, and I wouldn't trade it for the world. I have plenty of material things, much more than I deserve. I believe I am truly blessed beyond measure, but that is not what brings me happiness today. The things that mean the most to me don't have a price tag. My peace of mind and my purpose make me happy.

Today, I am in a position where I can introduce others to the solution I have been given. I have made many real friends along the way. The reason I say real friends is because I never really knew what that was before. I had plenty of associates with conditions, yet no one that was unconditional. During active addiction, I only hung out with drug addicts like myself.

Today, it is the same way, and the only difference is that we are no longer using it. They say you are like the people that you spend the most time with, and I spend time with people that are doing the right thing, and we have goals and ambitions. On the flip side, I know how to be a real friend today, and you attract what you are.

I am currently the director of a nonprofit called Pilgrim Progress, the same safe house that played a part in saving my life. All I want to do is share this gift of recovery that I have with others because it truly is a gift from above. I would never trade the life I have for anything. However, I know that if I don't continue to treat my disease on a daily basis, I will trade it for a bag or a bottle. Addiction is giving up everything for one thing, and recovery is giving up one thing for everything.

I hope this story inspires you in some way shape or form. If I can get sober anyone can with the help of God and a program. I don't regret any of the decisions I have made in my past or feel bad about any of the cards life had dealt me because they made me who I am today. My biggest liabilities have become my greatest assets. My experiences that were bad at the time are now the ones that I share with others so they can see that, no matter what has happened, they can be used for the good.

A wise man told me that not everyone shares my same experience, yet many will share the same feelings that I do. I hope no one reads this story and feels bad for me or has sad emotions. My story is one of a man that had some not-so-favorable circumstances which God used to help others.

Since I have been in recovery and have started living the life that God wants for me, many people cross my path that has shared similar experiences. I can let them know that I was in their shoes and that God currently uses my past to help others. I don't buy into coincidences; I think all things happen for a reason. We often don't understand why at the time, but looking back sometimes we can see things through a different lens.

Since I've been sober, my life hasn't always been perfect, but I know that, no matter what happens, there is no justifiable reason to get high. During active addiction, my brain told me the lie that when things happen, getting high will take the pain away, but it always made it worse. It is like putting a bandage on a bullet hole. Ironically people call those triggers, but I don't like the term. A trigger is on a gun, but if you don't pull the trigger, nothing happens. There is nothing in the world that can cause me to get high except for my decision to use.

I lost my father to this disease in July 2020. It was tough, but God was still there the whole time. I am glad that I was able to have a decent relationship with him and make amends before he passed. If I was in addiction, none of that would have happened.

Had it not been for others before me that shared their experience of losing a parent and staying sober, I'm not sure I would have been able to. I have also seen a lot of death from former clients and friends in recovery. This disease wants nothing more than to steal everything from us, especially our lives.

One of my biggest fears is relapse and what comes with it, and I know I am as susceptible as anyone else. As soon as I think that I'm in control, I know I'm in trouble. I don't believe I have this on lock, but I do have tools that I can utilize daily. Heavy emphasis on the daily part! I can't stay sober on yesterday's recovery. A smart man learns from his mistakes, but a wise man learns from the mistakes of others. I strive to be wise and always remain teachable.

All of the blessings that have come along with recovery are unreal. I have experienced things that I never could've imagined all by following God's purpose for me.

I have always wanted to travel the world to see what's out there. Since I have been sober, I have been overseas two times on mission trips. Although it had nothing to do with my career, I got the opportunity to help less fortunate people in Costa Rica. No matter what I do with the rest of my life, I want to help people in whatever way God sees fit.

Even in active addiction, I always felt like there was more to life than just working a job. I wanted to do something that would affect the grand scheme of things. I am truly blessed to have that opportunity today. I am only thirty years old, and I feel as if I have plenty of life left and many more things left to experience. Still, I know that tomorrow isn't promised.

In active addiction, I felt as if I wouldn't make it to thirty based on how I was living. Honestly, I didn't even want to live that long. The happiness that I have today is genuine, and I am truly grateful for the life I get to live. I no longer count the days; I try to make the days count. I believe that time is the most precious commodity in life. Anything you want in life can be achieved with the investment of time--education, relationships, careers, everything. So why would you waste such an important thing?

I have the career of my dreams right now all as a result of recovery and the life it has given to me. I have never had a job that was fulfilling before working in this field. I truly believe that I get the opportunity to do God's work! I have seen so many miracles in my life and the lives of others.

I get the opportunity to work with drug addicts and alcoholics as soon as they come out of detox and really feel hopeless. I introduce them to what recovery looks like, about how I was in the same situation not long ago, and that there is a solution. Then, a few months go by and you see a light come on where they really have hope and their lives begin restoration as well. There is nothing like it. Going from hopeless to hopeful is truly a miracle.

A week or a month may not seem like a long time in the grand scheme of things, but if you have been trapped in a prison in your own mind with an inevitable death sentence and no form of escape, any amount of time is freedom. If you are in recovery or addiction, you will know exactly what I am talking about. If not, imagine drowning underwater and, in the last second, you come up for air. It feels the same exact way. A breath of fresh air!

Any amount of time or effort is something to be proud of. Even if you don't succeed at first, as long as you try again and persevere through the hard times there is a lesson to be learned. No success story is without failures somewhere along the way. There is no testimony without tests. I have had a lot of friends relapse, but the blessed ones make it back.

If you are alive and reading this, you have a purpose and God wants to use you in some way. Just trust in Him, and you will realize your purpose. All things happen according to His plan. If things were meant to be another way, they would be. Even if you don't believe in recovery or God or anything you have read that's okay, just try to give recovery your best shot and see what happens.

I told myself when I came into recovery if what everyone was saying did not work, I would just go back to what I always did, but it has not let me down. I had nothing to lose and everything to gain with trying something different. Today I have everything to lose and nothing to gain if I pick up a drink or a drug.

I am truly grateful to be a part of this book. I hope I have said something somewhere along the way to help someone in some way. Simply put, if you want help just put in the footwork and you will get on the road to recovery. If you want what I have, do what I did to get it. If I can do it, so can you!

ABOUT THE AUTHOR:

Chase Campbell was born and raised in Rockingham, North Carolina. He is currently the director of a nonprofit organization called Pilgrims Progress that specializes in the recovery of people who suffer from addiction to drugs and alcohol. In 2020, Chase trained to become a North Carolina Certified Peer Support Specialist. He has also served overseas on mission trips to help the less fortunate in the slums of Costa Rica. He's been involved in mission trips on the east coast of the United States as well to help needy families affected by hurricane damage. Chase's primary focus in life is to help those that need it, especially people that have been down the same path as he has been with drug and alcohol addiction, and to show them that there is a way out.

HOW MY FATHER SAVED MY LIFE—TWENTY-FOUR YEARS AFTER HE DIED
Garry A. Carlson

I consider myself a legacy drunk, as I came by my disease honestly, and learned well from an active alcoholic father growing up. That's not to say that I always wanted to be an alcoholic, quite the contrary, I had resolved myself NOT to be one. But the nut, as they say, does not fall far from the tree.

First let me say that my father was NOT an abusive, raging maniac type of alcoholic. He was neither physically nor verbally abusive to anyone in our family. Rather he was a quiet drinker, trapped in his disease, up to the day he died from the complications associated with daily drinking for forty-plus years. Dad was just sixty years old when he died, and I was eighteen.

My father experienced the ravages of daily alcoholic drinking on his liver and kidneys and had undergone some previous minor treatments for those organs when they raged against him. But that did not stop him from continuing to drink. One fateful day, November 30, 1970—his liver exploded. The tall stoic man shrunk, crumpling to a puddle on the floor, with blood rushing from his mouth. I was standing right there in my kitchen, in shock, to witness this event.

EMTs rushed him to our local hospital where the doctors

valiantly performed nothing short of a miracle by stopping the bleeding and pseudo-repairing his liver. All was well they felt, and he went from the surgery suite into the recovery room to slowly reawaken back to consciousness. But there in the recovery room, as they were bringing Dad off sedation, his body went into serious convulsions, known as the DT's (Delirium Tremors), from withdrawal from alcohol. All of the miracle surgery and doctors could not stop the inevitable, and he died right there in the recovery room of the hospital.

My shock at the finality of this moment was twofold; the reality of this disease caught up to my father—so then, I wasn't ultimately surprised. Over the years I had heard my mother plead with him to go get help. Alcoholics Anonymous was available at that point and was a proven commodity for those who had a desire to stop drinking alcohol. The signposts were there for him—I guess—and for me as well. I realized the truth about what alcohol can and will do to you if you drink daily on that fateful day in November 1970.

Another signpost he must have seen was the fact that six months before his death, my father's older brother, who lived in Sweden, at age sixty-three, hung himself because he just could not stop drinking.

I had consciously watched the disease ravage my dad, since I was about five or six, asking my mother then "Why does Daddy have to drink his coffee from a saucer and not a cup?"

My mother explained that his hands shook so much in the morning hours that he would spill most of the cup before it ever touched his lips. I was a spectator in a living horror film for the next thirteen years. I became, by default, an expert observer.

I never really wanted to drink, at all, through my high school years. Or participate in any marijuana-related relief, as THAT was plentiful during the late '60s.

It wasn't until my father died in 1970, that I vowed: "Never to become the man that he had become."

Easier said than done.

I started smoking pot right after he died, rationalizing that the

Marijuana Maintenance plan would offer me a safe alternative to alcohol. For me, as it turned out, that was about as safe of a decision as would have been buying a first-class ticket on the Titanic!! Turns out in the long run, I ended up in the same place.

About two months after his death, I enlisted in the US Air Force and had a choice of what job I would have. The Vietnam War was raging, and the draft was an ongoing threat for all eighteen to twenty-five-year-old young men. My enlisting afforded me choices of a specialty occupation. This is as opposed to getting drafted as another basic infantry soldier. In recovery circles, we call that a geographic cure. The main challenge with a geographic cure is that wherever I go, there I am. And I am the common denominator to all of my problems. So, I might have changed my address but I still brought the entirety of my problems and their faulty habits with me. Willingly or not, I was running away from a situation right into the arms of my disease.

You see, although the legal drinking age in Massachusetts in 1971 was twenty-one when you are just nineteen and, in the military, —you can buy and consume 3.2% alcohol beer—with a proper Military ID. With my ID in hand, I was off and running. My peers all engaged in daily drinking and a few smoked weed as well. I felt right at home in this environment.

I was lucky that they valued the electronics training I got in high school. I excelled at my nine months of radio maintenance training in Mississippi, and I was a hit at my first duty station in Maine. So much so, they sent me back to Mississippi for advanced training three months after I arrived there. All the while, I was drinking lots of beer and smoking pot, yet maintaining a good work record and responsibility for the most part.

This behavior went on and steadily increased over the next twenty-two years or so. My employment was steady with no DWIs, totaled cars, or people hurt. All things being equal, I am not proud to say my arrest was certain IF I was ever stopped, on a great many occasions.

Jump ahead twenty-four years, and five days after my father's death, I am married now and have two teenaged children. I am still drinking and have known for years I have a problem, just like my dad did. I had bottles of liquor hidden in several places in my house, just like my dad. By then I was also a daily drinker, just like my dad. When I looked in the mirror sometimes, I saw my dad there. It had been gnawing on my subconscious for about fifteen years or so, knowing that I WAS just like my father.

But on this day, I get up with a steadfast resolve that I need to STOP drinking, or else. This was my tipping point, for no particular reason, I just woke up with this sense of urgency to STOP drinking, right now! I tell people that I got tired of seeing my dad's face in the mirror every morning. My failure was at NOT being the man he was, but I was very successful at duplicating his exact demeanor and modality. I called central service AA in Boston and they gave me a list of four night-time meetings I could attend, and they would mail me a comprehensive listing of meetings all around my hometown. The date of my first ever AA meeting was December 5th, 1994.

I attended my first meeting that night and felt strangely comfortable in this room of thirty or so people, none of whom I knew. But still, I felt a connection or belonging there. I didn't speak but I listened intently and learned some things. I knew I wanted to come back the next day and learn more.

I drove home, told my wife what I saw and felt about the meeting, and then retired early that night. Seems I couldn't wait until "tomorrow" so I could go to my 2nd ever AA meeting. I did NOT have a drink as was customary for me to do EVERY night. I never even opened the refrigerator to look for a beer. This was my first full day of recovery.

My wife at the time gave me a mixed message about my drinking after arriving home from this first meeting. Although she had been occasionally vocal about something I did or said under the influence of alcohol over the past five years or so, she was now telling me that I am not an alcoholic and that I don't need to attend those meetings!

Instead, she said, "You just need to drink a little less. What do those people know about you?"

She continued quizzing me saying that she doesn't like it when I refer to myself as an alcoholic. My former wife also told me that she didn't want the kids to hear me say that about myself.

I didn't buy into that perspective. Lucky for me I believed that I was, just like my father, a full-fledged, card-carrying, alcoholic and thus fully qualified to be a member of AA. I went to my second meeting the next night, and my first miracle happened. It may not seem like that big of a deal to you, but for me, an alcoholic and daily drinker, this was a huge non-event.

Because I was only given a brief list of four meetings, one each for Monday-Thursday, I was very dismayed to find that the meeting on Tuesday night was no longer at THAT address!! I double and triple-checked the address, and sure enough, I was there, but the lights were all off and the doors were locked. I briefly thought about breaking into the building, because I felt that the sobriety I was looking for was in THAT locked building. I thought it through and did not break into the building. Instead, I accepted that I would have to wait until the Wednesday meeting to get my next dose of sobriety and recovery.

What about the miracle I hear you saying? Well, for me to drive home, I had to physically drive past three different liquor stores, all of which I frequented on different days of the week, otherwise, someone might get the idea that I was an alcoholic!! The fact was, exactly that. I WAS an active alcoholic, and the miracle was that I did not throw in the towel and say "screw-it, I guess it wasn't to be," and go get drunk.

No, I didn't do that at all, and I wholeheartedly feel that the fact that I had enough resolve and belief in my conviction to stop drinking and drive past those liquor stores. To me, that absolutely WAS a miracle. Nothing less than that. There would be, as I found out, many more miracles to follow. In hindsight, it seems to me as though I had received a dose of sobriety and stick to-it-tiveness at that first meeting to carry me through for two days. That was a major ingredient in that first miracle!

In my first 90 days of recovery & sobriety, I met some incredibly generous people who helped me get my feet planted and my head on straight. (They gave to me freely what was freely given to them!) In hindsight, I realized, sometime later on during that time, (~90 days) that I had developed four distinct cornerstones to my temple of sobriety, serenity, and peace. They were:

A.) I got a sponsor; (Cornerstone Column #1 of my Sobriety) In my experience, getting a sponsor was NOT rocket science, and it is extremely important to have a sponsor ASAP. I believe that I asked my first sponsor, Dennis, to be my sponsor twelve days after coming to my first meeting. I had heard him speak at two meetings and I liked what he shared. He had also identified himself as an available sponsor.

When choosing a sponsor, to begin with, we don't have to be a perfect match. It's a TEMPORARY sponsorship we are entering into, not a marriage. My sponsor Dennis was an incredibly calming influence for me, as I wanted everything to happen quickly, today, right now! He told me, in a very matter-of-fact tone, that TIME was the tool I should be using to gauge my level of recovery.

He advised me that TIME was an acronym that meant "Things I Must Earn."

All things in recovery take TIME to develop. I believed him and I learned that day to be a little more patient about my expectations.

I committed to a suggestion from my sponsor that I try to attend 90 meetings in 90 days. I did agree and believe that I had gone to more than one-hundred meetings in the first ninety days. I woke up every day setting myself up for success by anchoring my day around the meeting I was going to go to that day or evening. For me, I am a numbers guy and goal-driven so this suggestion was easy to follow.

My sponsor suggested I become involved in in-service work as my home group's coffee maker about six weeks in. Another opportunity to commit to my program. I would have to arrive thirty minutes early to make the coffee and help with the room setup. People in that meeting, about fifty all told, were counting on me to make the coffee, so I better be there. I was engaged in this group, and they, in turn, were engaged in my recovery.

What I learned in those first 90 days with my sponsor, is that when your sponsor makes a suggestion, you should go out and do that suggestion, no questions asked. You must have a little faith in your sponsor and if you don't then, well, maybe it's time to look for a new sponsor. But my point here is that what I came to understand about suggestions, is simply this. You won't ever understand the value of the suggestion until AFTER you have done the suggestion. THEN and only then could I see the wisdom in taking that action. For me, after I did only two or three simple suggestions, without question, I had immense faith and confidence in my sponsor's ability to guide me. Dennis was the first of many awesome sponsors I have had in twenty-six years. I don't ever want to be without a sponsor as they are lifesavers for sure.

B.) I started attending a very large Men's Meeting called TSDD (Cornerstone Column #2 of my Sobriety).

I believe that it was the 17th day of sobriety that someone suggested to me, (not my sponsor) that I check out a Men's Group called TSDD. That name stood for "Tough Shit Don't Drink" and as you might figure they had a philosophy about never having to take another drink ever again. No matter what!

On my 21st day of sobriety, I went to check out this Men's Meeting. I was more than a little intimidated by the line of fully dressed, Harley Davidson-dressed motorcycles parked out front. I wondered what I was walking into there and I was very much outside of my comfort zone. But I somehow felt comfortable enough to walk into the building and observed over one-hundred men all talking with great enthusiasm and laughter in their expression, before the meeting began. When the meeting began, they were all business and took their responsibilities very seriously.

I wanted to learn more about this process and so I took a seat and leaned in. I was all-in in an hour and a half, and hardly ever missed a meeting in the next 90 days of my sobriety. During my first meeting, I was gently nudged to go pick up a 1-29 days coin and ultimately be recognized for my courage to stop drinking. The applause I got for doing that was deafening. The congratulatory response was infectious.

I wanted more of this, and so I followed the rule of thumb is 12-step recoveries, which was, "If you want what we have then come to do what we do!"

I was going to do exactly that, by following their example, and stay sober another week, and keep returning to the TSDD meetings. Don't get me wrong, I had my share of challenges during the first few years. But the power in the grounding of my feet and emotions by this group of men was hugely impactful towards my continued sobriety. I had a connection to this group even when I was away on business and had to miss a weekly meeting. I WAS there in spirit and would act to protect my sobriety another week until I could return to the TSDD Meeting. (But I also attended several other meetings during the week as well.)

These men had recovered and were happy, joyful, and free. But they were diligent about the perils that lurked just outside the walls.

Someone there told me, "Just because the monkey is off your back doesn't mean the circus has left town! That alcoholic/addiction gorilla is outside your door, pumping iron and just waiting for you to leave the door ajar, so he can kick it in."

I knew that once inside this gorilla would kick my ass, and I would be trying to get one day sober all over again. Some people don't ever get back what they had, and they perish. I didn't want to be a statistic of alcohol or addiction and I learned from these men how to 'cowboy up' regarding my sobriety.

C.) Realized that there were people around me who wanted me to **FAIL** at staying sober, hence it strengthened my resolve to succeed long term (Cornerstone Column #3 of my Sobriety).

This was a little bit crazy but oh so common for us humans. When people close to us want to make a change and we don't want them to be different, we will act, unconsciously, to sabotage their progress. Well, I had someone in my life who did NOT want me to get and stay sober and they told me so, many times in my 90 days and all through my first year of sobriety.

That reaction to my best efforts and intentions, caused me to double down on my efforts and my conviction to my sobriety, as tender as it was. I was up for the fight of (and for) my life it seemed, and I was NOT going to succumb to the prison confines of this disease, and I pushed back. Hard.

The fact was that as little time as I had achieved, I remembered that I had escaped from my alcoholic prison and could not let anything or anyone deter me from my goal of No More Drinking or Recreational Drug Use. Period. **No Matter What!**

D.) Came to realize at around my 90th day of sobriety, that thirty-six years earlier, my father had said to me, when I was just five to six years old, something that would solidify my commitment to my long-term sobriety like nothing else could. (Cornerstone Column #4 of my sobriety)

This one event, remembering *this* conversation, was the first huge miracle that I had in recovery, and that one thing has been my rock-solid foundation to my continued, day-to-day fight to stay sober another day. Just one more day. The words that follow here are the telling core of this entire story.

When I was five years old or so, my parents and I were visiting my aunt and uncle. My Uncle Andy was also an immigrant Swede, like my father, who had married my mother's sister. My dad and uncle liked to sit in the kitchen and spend time drinking beer and whiskey. So, whenever they needed another beer from the fridge, they called on the best little beer runner there was in sight, "ME" and I was happy to oblige.

This was 1957 mind you, so "pop-top" cans hadn't been invented yet, so you had to use a "church-key" can and bottle opener. These had a pointed end in which you pierced the top of the can in TWO places and then the beer would then pour out nicely. I had tried to open a can of beer a few times before but just couldn't get the leverage to pierce the tin can.

On this day, however, I DID manage to open the can and I was beside myself with my newfound strength and recent world title for youngest ever beer can opener.

I remarked to my dad with great enthusiasm, "I did it, daddy, I am so strong!!"

He quietly leaned over and whispered in my ear, "Someday soon, I hope you will grow up and be so strong—you will never open a can of beer ever again."

BAM! Like a sudden flash of lightning—this was THE major cornerstone of my sobriety. That message from my father had resided in my subconscious for about thirty-six years, and I don't believe I ever gave it a conscious thought. But when I realized and remembered the conversation, it was massively, profoundly, impactful for me. My father was speaking to me, and I knew I had to listen. If my other three cornerstones were made from concrete and rebar steel, THIS cornerstone was made of titanium!!!

I knew that this was a life and death situation, because, as I said, I am a legacy drunk. I knew what could and would happen if I continued drinking as I was every day. I would find a reason to drink no matter what. I had personally watched the horror this disease had over my father and he just couldn't stop. It literally killed him. My disease wanted (and STILL wants!!) to continually take from me until I am either institutionalized, imprisoned, or dead. That's what my experience of twenty-six years spoke to me, and I know that this is true.

When I mentioned that I am a legacy drunk and that this issue for me is life or death, that is spot on how I feel about my disease. It IS Life or Death for me, and most likely YOU too if you are reading this.

Early on in my sobriety, people told me to prepare myself for the bodies I would have to step over, from people who just didn't get the seriousness of this disease. I have had to do exactly that, and NOT drink because of it. In my first seven years of sobriety, I had to endure a divorce, my older brother Buddy, passing due to his diabetes, and my older sister Carol passing due to cancer. I never drank through any of that, although my disease would have loved it if I did!

Instead, I simply (NOT easy, but simply) utilized the tools and people of my recovery community around me, and I got through it all. Add to that a passing of a dear friend, Scott W., who just could not get any long-term sobriety from drugs and alcohol. As much as I wanted him to succeed, he didn't have the ambition or drive and he overdosed on heroin, one time too many. That was nineteen years ago. To this day I am still so angry at his disease—he had so much to live for. Scott was a very talented and accomplished carpenter. He was a good man—and my friend.

But it's not up to me to keep others sober. It is up to me however to help other alcoholics whenever I see the need for helping another. That's the 12th step at work and I have to be available to help if I am asked or if I see the need. I must give away that which was freely given to me. I don't need to go on a recruiting program trying to save the world. This 12-step program's design is to grow by attraction and not promotion. It is very successful for people who WANT it, not those who need it. That's not my call.

Writing my story as I have, will hopefully connect with others that may want to make a change to what is controlling them, and I pray that it will help somebody. I will tell you that you CAN do this process even when the voices in your head tell you that you can't. There is a life out there that you are meant to live, and you can get out of that wretched existence of addiction if you want to. No one else can do the work for you, however; it just doesn't work that way.

Sobriety is not a spectator event. You must get into action and work for your peace of mind, body, and spiritual connection. You cannot think your way into right acting but you can act your way into right thinking. Go out and get connected to whatever means are available to you and stop the cycle. Just for one day, TODAY. Repeat the process tomorrow. Keep it simple.

I am a few months away from my 70th birthday, and my life is full of richness and is bountiful. I am grateful for all that I have in my life today, and I am not afraid to express my gratitude to my Higher Power and those around me. Although I am not a millionaire, I do have things that no amount of money could ever buy. I have peace in my life today and a very grateful heart. I have twenty-six years of continuous, non-stop sobriety. To me, my sobriety is simply priceless! You can't buy it, and I can't sell it either. The ONLY way you can get it is to EARN IT, one day at a time!

I find it ironic that my father LOST his LIFE in the RECOVERY room after surgery—while I found the gift of my LIFE in the RECOVERY rooms of AA.

Not only did I find my life, the one I deserved, but I found a life immensely better than anything I thought I would ever or could ever have. I have people, places, and things in my life today that frankly, I don't think I deserve. However, I will accept that I do deserve them, or else why would they be present in my life today? I am tremendously blessed and I know it.

My blessing and hope for your lives is this simple desire and tasking. May you find everything you need to recover from drugs and alcohol—including meeting with like-minded, caring, and loving people. This happened to me almost twenty-six years ago. I know that you CAN do this. It is NOT easy, but it is simple.

The fact is that twenty-six years AFTER I stepped into my first AA meeting, I am still witnessing rooms and zooms full of like-minded, caring, loving people, who want to share their experience, strength, and hope with others who need to know that "Yes You CAN do this!" I am not shy about being proud to be a long-term recovered alcoholic. I pray that this story may be beneficial, in some way or another, to you or someone close to you.

So that's my story about how my father spoke to me twenty-four years after his death, and how what he said helped to save this legacy alcoholic's life.

Thanks, Daddy!

ABOUT THE AUTHOR:

Garry A. Carlson is a speaker, business coach, author, and youth services volunteer who strives to make a difference in the lives and paths that he crosses. His unceasingly dedicated optimism and gratitude have been crucial to his success in recovery and pass that along to those he coaches, speaks to, and counsels. Gary's philosophy of 'Gratitude is _the_ key ingredient for a Great Attitude' has provided many with a new perspective and ability for individuals to make lasting changes in their lives.

ONE MORE DAY
Derrick L. Pearson

"Honey, something is wrong. I can't breathe," I said.

No breath means no life, and I could not breathe. How did I get to this? What to do next?

The words stopped us in our tracks. These words are a call to the bat signal. Help is required. But let's not go there, yet. Most journeys are a combination of turns and a change of direction. This was a redirection. For redirection to happen, friction must exist. This was friction. Let's walk back in time together.

January 2016. The Woodlands, Texas. I was coaching high school basketball at The John Cooper School. The team had just spent a week in San Diego playing in a holiday tournament, and when I got picked up from the airport, my body failed me. It was not working. There had not been any MOMENT that led to the injury. There had been several silent moments, an accumulation of moments, which led to the pain I was feeling. I could not recall any falls or bumps or jumps that would lead to this pain, but it was an "injury" pain rather than an "I am hurt" pain.

Athletes and coaches know the difference. They know what I mean by it. As a player or coach, we learn to access pain by asking "are you hurt or are you injured?" It's the intersection for what is done next. Are you hurt or are you injured? Hurt is temporary pain due to impact or discomfort. Hurt is a stinger that was due to impact, or the reaction to a big hit in football. Injured are the long-term and permanent friction that will require a change in action and reaction. Hurt means I can keep going. Injured means let's evaluate the situation and do something about it. I was injured.

I did a mental recall of the previous week and there was nothing. No hint to injury and no clue as to its cause. It was just THERE. Loud. Constant. Pain. I had been hurt many times and had built up what I thought was a toughness to it, from it.

I had used the phrase "I have a super high pain threshold." As if I said it enough it would be true.

"I'm okay."

"I'll be fine."

Except for THIS time. I was not okay. I was injured. This deserved my attention. Off to the doctor, I went.

Hospital emergency room. X-rays. Pain meds. Rest. Ice. Repeat. Don't work. Stay home. Let it recover. Let IT recover. Back spasms? Muscle sprain? Pain meds. Ice. Repeat. Don't work. Stay home. Let it recover. None of this helped. I remained in pain. I also kept coaching. I wanted to finish the job. I needed to finish the season. There was half a season left. My guys needed me. I would trudge ahead, pain be damned. I would medicate at night, ice all day, and then head to practice or games. Repeat. The pain was constant. Are you hurt or are you injured? I was injured but acting hurt. Stupid ego.

"Go to a specialist," my wife demanded.

"Why? They are only going to tell me the same thing and do the same stuff!" I said stubbornly.

Finally, after a road game where the bumpy bus ride was too much to bear, I agreed to see a specialist. Spasms and strain. Heavier meds and more ice. I had been validated. "See?" "Told you!" I would just have to tough it out. Back to practice. Back to games. Coaching. Teaching. Loving. Here's the thing about pain. It does not care about what you think you must do. It cares not about your ego or what you want to do.

Pain said "Oh, so you are trying to ignore my warnings? Well, how about THIS level of pain?" Stupid ego.

The morning after a night game, I slept in and went to make coffee. I attempted to bend over, and the pain announced its presence with authority.

"SIR, I HAVE ASKED FOR YOUR CONSIDERATION AND YOU HAVE IGNORED ME, SO NOW I MUST HUMBLE YOU!" (You should read that in the voice of James Earl Jones because that is how I believe the voice of God sounds like)

"KNEEL BEFORE ME!"

I took a knee and could not get up. I tried to pull up on the sink, but the pain did what felt like a victory lap up and down my leg. It knocked me flat onto the kitchen floor, and let me tell you, this was humbling indeed. I could not move. I could not reach for the phone. I could not pull myself up. It was just me and the mat in front of the sink. Oh, and the ceiling. I got familiar with the kitchen ceiling. Did you know that if one is to ever believe that their kitchen is clean, they should lay on their back, flat as a board, and look at the underside of your cabinets? Oh, and let me give you this bit of advice from this former floor dweller, there really is a cool element to being on the kitchen tile. It is cooler than anything in your house. Three degrees cooler. Carry on.

It took me about an hour to be able to roll over to my side and find a way to my feet. I need to thank my Algebra teacher and coach, Fran Imbrescia because I think I may have been found on that very kitchen floor some eight hours later had I not reached back to some algebraic equation to determine the proper angle required to get me to my side and push off the cabinet and get to my feet. Thank you, Coach! Appreciated. Now, let me say this, I made some sounds in getting to my side that would best be described as wounded warthog meets growling grizzly bear. I immediately understood the sounds my stepdad made when getting up off a soft couch when he got older. Frightening.

I called my wife and simultaneously called my physician to explain my ridiculous floor morning. I was referred to another specialist, who set an appointment for that afternoon. It wasn't really an appointment. It was more like stalking the two o'clock part of the day when I knew they would not be available after 3 pm. I gingerly walk myself into their office and immediately they huddle and whisper. I am told to get into a wheelchair and was wheeled to the medical center next door. MRIs and more pictures of me in various pretzel-like torturous poses.

"Can you move your knee up some, Sir?"

"If I could, do you think I would be here on this table?"

"Right."

After twelve requests to move and twelve refusals, the technician finally goes with taking the video and pictures as is. "Hmmm." "Oh." "Wow!" Not exactly what you want to hear from medical professionals. I ask what was seen and no answers were given. Finally, I am wheeled back to the office and a meeting of minds took place.

"You have a fracture on your spine, and you have some nerve irritation. We think some shots will help you feel better."

"Wait, a fracture?" was my response.

I had been walking around with a fractured spine. I did not want surgery. Spinal injections were suggested. Injections. Into my spine. Whoa. Giving my spine to someone was a matter of trust and faith. I would not go easily into this thing, but I was convinced that it would be better than not.

I began getting spinal injections and I would take the shot and then go and coach. I had parents bring pillows to put in my chair so that I could sit and coach. My players would run up to me so that I could stay seated. Officials would walk up to me to discuss fouls and rules. It was brutal. It was also better than it was. I made it through the season and thought I was on the mend. So much so that I decided to go straight into baseball season the day after basketball ended. I was given an assistant who would hit infield and who would run practices as I stood or sat and bellowed from a distance. I made it through several weeks of painfilled baseball practices and games. This team was playing well, and I loved leading them.

In the next to last game, I was coaching third with a runner on base. One of my players hit a line drive down the line RIGHT AT ME. Stiff. Sore. In pain. I had to decide. Get out of the way or take the line drive. I matrix-dove in slow motion as the ball missed me by inches. There I was, flat on my stomach in the third-base coaching box. I did a body parts check laying face down. What hurts? What works? What to do now? How in the world am I going to get up? Thankfully, my team sprinted out of the dugout to help me up. Pretty embarrassing. Very humbling. I finished the game and the season. I also went back to the specialist.

I was referred to an NFL doctor and he suggested more videos and more pictures. I harumphed and complained that this is horrible. Finally, I agreed to more torture in the MRI space. A few days later I get that call that makes your skin crawl.

"Can you please come into the office so that we can discuss what we found?"

Those calls are the WORST. I agreed and was met with some awful news. Along with that fracture on my spine was ANOTHER spine fracture! But the greater pain was coming from what had just been found. I had two herniated discs in my back. I had taken all those horrible shots directly in my spine and had been misdiagnosed. He sent me to a top surgeon for an opinion, and spinal fusion surgery was recommended. Again, I would have to ponder allowing access to my SPINE. This time, I had to consider my SPINAL CORD. I was not comfortable with it. I was less comfortable with the pain. I had to decide.

I needed approval from my insurance company, and they took their good ole time in getting back to the doctor. One week passed. Then another, and then another. Finally, I called the insurance company and found out that not only had they screwed up, but the surgeon's office has as well. Had I not called, I might still be waiting for surgery approval. FINALLY, I got verbal approval and the surgery was scheduled. Or so I thought. Another screw-up in the coding for the procedure forced another two-week delay. The surgery was going to happen. I was scared. It was my spine, and I had to put aside my human doubt and embrace my trust in my faith.

The hospital was about five minutes from my house, so it was a short trip. I had a history of not responding to anesthesia. Once, I had awakened during surgery on my hand and foot earlier, and they had to add more or a stronger dose to knock me out. During the hand surgery, I woke up mid-surgery and spoke to the medical staff that it was cool for them to let me watch the surgery on someone else's hand. I took the IVs, kissed my wife, and prayed. I couldn't wait to wake up. I put on my headphones, queued up my Best of Fred Hammond playlist, and was off to dreamland.

I woke from surgery and was still not alert. I had made it through. My wife and the nurse told me that it had been an exceedingly long procedure. All I wanted to know was if I was going to be okay. They said yes, BUT…

Whoa. What do you mean, BUT? I needed a catheter. I had been PUNCTURED during its insertion. WHAT?!! I had every fear of what allowing a human to have access to my spine could mean. I had thought every thought about what could, should, and BETTER happen. Nowhere in my thoughts in prayers was a catheter or issues from one. My urethra was punctured.

Can I take a moment and discuss catheters? Male catheters are NO JOKE. I had never considered them until I woke up with one still attached to me. This thing had a bag stuck to my upper thigh. That's one thing. The real thing is that the other end of it was still attached to me from the inside of me. THERE. Look, I had no idea what other people knew about this, but this thing was attached to the inside of me in a very delicate place. How can I say this? Every time I moved my leg, this thing PULLED on where I was attached to it. HARD. Remember the pain in my back? It was NOTHING compared to the pull of this thing. I asked what was next and they said I need to heal THERE first. Let me tell you, this is pain. And this is awkward. Oh yeah. My spine.

This punctured urethra thing had become another obstacle. More pain. More restrictions. More healing. More friction. I was told that I needed to heal and then learn to use the bathroom again. I had to learn to roll over, stand up, squat, and walk again. I had to commit to a body cast that prevents bending. I had to wear this contraption for months. I had to learn everything. Basic human stuff. Sigh. Okay, let's go.

I began with the basics and progressed to walking with a walker around the hospital floor. I finally got clearance to go home after a few days. Lots of rules to follow. Get up on the hour and move around. Hydrate. Rest. Take the prescribed meds. Don't bend or get the areas wet. Protect your spine. Do as you are told. Home, sweet home. Time to get better.

The morning after I got home, I slowly manipulated my frame to my walker and proceeded to laps around the first-floor level of the house. After a few laps, I recognized that I was struggling to breathe. It was like wet cotton was filling my lungs. Every breath became more difficult, and each breath felt like I was closer to not having another breath.

"Honey, something is wrong. I can't breathe."

There are several moments in this thing that jump out to me. First, my wife saved my life several times. Once it was in acting quickly, another was in holding me up, and another will be discussed later.

On this day, as soon as I said I couldn't breathe, she called my surgeon. IMMEDIATELY. She was told to call 911 and get me to the hospital as quickly as possible. She calmly hung up, dialed 911, and began gathering herself for this next thing to come. I suffer from sleep apnea. I use a c-pap machine that helps my breathing, especially when my allergies back up on me, so my immediate thought was to put the mask on to see if it would help force air into my lungs. It did. Remember "are you hurt or are you injured?"

I was injured. As a coach, when players would have difficulty breathing, I would suggest standing up straight and focusing on air in and air out. I thought about laying down, but then I recalled my own words. Straighten and stand up. Mask on. Focus. Air in. Air out. Air in. Air out.

Five minutes later, the EMTs and firemen showed up at my door and in my bedroom. My wife had prepared them for me by telling them what had happened, and this allowed them to act quickly, professionally, and expertly. It's almost as though they knew what was happening. An IV was put in and I was gently put on the stretcher and into the back of the ambulance. Air in. Air out. Focus. I watched my neighbors as they watched me. I could do nothing for myself except focus. Air in. Air out. I looked at my wife and tears began to roll down my face. How could this be happening? How could I leave her behind? The siren sounds, and off we go.

It's a quick five minutes to the emergency entrance of the same hospital where my surgery was performed. My surgeon was there waiting for me. It's as if he knew what was happening. He had a team of people with him and Beckie listened as they discussed what happened, and what was happening. Several discussions and I seemed to start dreaming. I was listening to conversations about me as if I was not there. Beckie asked questions. The surgeon asked questions. There were more questions than answers. I was in the hallway now, laying there listening. Listening. Looking at myself and listening to everything.

I woke up to a new face, and then another new face. A nurse and another doctor. They were huddled up pondering loudly about a person who could hear them. "What do we do?" "Isn't that risky?" I heard phrases like spinal hemorrhaging and blood work. I must be honest and tell you all that I was not alert or on top of most of the goings-on for that day. I just knew that a few doctors were working on me and several nurses. I know that my wife held my hand a lot, and I would fall asleep and wake up often. I was then told that I needed to be wheeled into be scanned. I had no idea what for, but I knew that the man who was sent into the room to scan me had no time or desire to share who he was, what he was looking for, or what it meant. All I know is that he did that thing…" Hmmm" "okay" and "well." I asked him if he could share what he saw, and he ignored me and left the room. Okay cool, no resting now. It was stress time.

I waited. And, waited. Finally, my doctor came in and delivered the news.

"You have blood clots. When you hear of people passing away after surgery, it's often due to a blood clot. You have blood clots."

I replied, "Hold up Doc, you said clots. Plural. One can kill you. How many do I have?"

He said, "Twenty-eight."

Let that one marinate for a second. One can kill you. I had twenty-eight.

The doctor continued, "You have three in your heart. You have four in your lungs. The twenty are in your legs. That's twenty-seven. They brought along a bully. It's called a saddle embolism. Imagine a saddle, and it has wrapped itself around your bronchial stem to choke you to death."

Well, how about that? This thing let the clots into my heart and lungs and NOW is trying to choke me to death.

I have lived a full life. I was comfortable saying before the surgery that if God took me tomorrow, I have lived several lifetimes worth. But on THAT day, I was praying a different song. "I know I said I'd be okay if you took me tomorrow, but if you don't mind, I wouldn't mind staying a while longer."

I asked what was next. Whew. I did not expect to hear what I was told.

"Well, we are afraid to treat the clots because the thinner could hemorrhage your spine from the surgery and you would die. If we don't treat it, well, you could die that way too."

I did not know what to say. Finally, one of the doctors said that of the four doctors in the discussion and treatment, none of them had a patient who had survived that many blood clots OR a saddle embolism. WHAT?! Right about then, another one of the doctors told my wife that they would proceed with the blood thinners and put a filter in to try and catch any clot that broke free. I was told that they would enter through either my neck or my groin to run the filter through, and I immediately demanded that they go through my

NECK. Leave my groin alone. Another procedure. More prayers. More stress.

I was also told that these things could get you in your sleep, so I was afraid to sleep. The meds made me sleepy, and I was now afraid to sleep. At that moment, I asked for one more day. Please wake me up. Please wake me up. Please wake me up.

I woke up in the middle of the night and a nurse began preparing me for the next procedure. Hospital televisions in the ICU are hilarious. Middle of the night, wifey and I are trying to distract ourselves with bad tv, and here come the insanely inappropriate ads about filters and lawsuits. We looked at each other and howled in laughter. What was going on? This tv ran these ads every break, so we saw it A LOT. We laughed every time we saw it. She told me to go to my go-through, which was headphones, Fred Hammond, and a kiss.

I woke up an hour later and they took me down to put in the filter. I had a video message from my friend Griff. He said, "You are already healed, Homie!" I cried. I also had a voice message from my older brother who said, "God put you in the right place, at the right time, and the right people to heal you."

I cried more. They were both JUST what I needed.

I woke from surgery and thanked the Lord for one more day. I was now with the catheter, the body cast, the filter in my heart, and the thing in my neck. I could not walk, stand, rollover, or bend. I simply was. I looked over at my wife, the most soldier of all soldiers, sleeping cramped up on the couch in my ICU room. The chaplain visited frequently, holding not only my hand—but my soul. I listened to Fred, laughed at those awful commercials, and got talked and hand-washed through it all by an angelic nurse who learned every part of me with care.

This nurse stayed with me. She bathed me, cleaned me up, and rewrapped me. She talked to my wife and whispered in my ear that it was going to be okay. She told me about her husband and her kids and asked about my daughter and my teams. She along with the chaplain delivered me from hour to hour. I began to pout, being frustrated with immobility and the inability to be human. I mention those angels to mention another. There was my wife, the surgeon, the nurses, my homie, my brother, the chaplain, this nurse, and MARY.

Mary and I went to school together as kids, and we had been reconnected recently as she traveled to work in Houston. We met up, laughed, smiled ear to ear, and hugged. Mary has such a special spirit and as friends go, she is unique in her goodness. Mary found out what I was going through and was going to be in town again while I was in ICU. She set some things aside and came to the ICU and visited me. As important was the fact that she visited my wife as well. She gave us both her smile and hugs, Mary shared her love and left us better than she found us. One of my favorite pictures is the one of me in the ICU room chair, getting out of bed to do so, sandwiched in between two angels, my wife, and my Mary. I will never be able to repay her for what she did and how she did it. I hope that I have told her so. Thank you.

I finally managed to get moved from ICU, and into a private room. New nurses. New restrictions. New directions. I must admit, having the catheter removed while awake is one of my least favorite things ever. EVER. Thanks to social media, I got to share my love with my friends. I tried to thank them for the love that they showered upon me over my time in ICU and after. I have the best family and friends, and a million thanks would not be enough.

I finally got to go home a few days later, and I had my playbook. I also had my fears. More importantly, I had my faith. I heard the words of my wife, my loving mother-in-law, my daughter, and my friends. My mother-in-law was tasked with stopping by and making sure that I ate, slept, and had someone to love on me. My wife worked from home as much as possible, and I had nurses stop by daily to help. I had to re-learn walking, so I started with a walker around the house, which led to one day using it outside of the house on my street. I had to put my ego aside and learn to do what was needed rather than what I wanted to. After a week or so of using the walker, I pushed it aside in favor of a walking cane instead to walk my block.

It went from one lap to two, two to four, and four to fifteen. The neighbors cheered me on as I slowly, meticulously made my way around the neighborhood circle, day after day, night after night. One day, my wife came home from work and my grin made her ask what I was smiling for.

I said, "don't be mad but I left the neighborhood and walked down the street on the walking path!"

I had put the cane down and moved forward. That became a mile a day, to two, to four, to ten. Step by step, day by day, get better and better!

Another angel to note was Brodie. He was my best friend during all of this. Brodie was a recovering rescue who arrived right before my surgery, who needed love. We loved on him as we had him forever, and he loved us back with all of his puppy heart. He had a rough surgery and it seemed like he understood when I was in pain and wasn't feeling well. After Brody's and my surgery—we took on the journey of healing together. He would lay on the bed, head on my arm, staring at me with those beautiful brown eyes. Brodie was amazing. He knew how I felt and never pushed or wavered. If I felt awful, he would hold that signal to go potty until my wife or mom-in-law walked in. He would look at me as if asking how are we doing today? Is this a walk day? Is this a stay in bed day? No matter what, he was okay with whatever needed to be done that day. Some say we saved him. I can say that he helped save me.

Once I started walking, I started receiving visitors from all over the country. To Mary, Barbara, Mom Barbara and Holly, Bill, Helen, and my best friend Lossie, a million thank-you's are not enough for what you did and who you are. You gave up your time and came to hang out with me in my toughest of times.

I want to thank my angels, my friends, for my community of amazing human beings, and the people who love me consistently, constantly, and out loud.

Since those days, I have redirected my life and my energy. I learned to filter my lungs, clear my heart, and extend my stride. I learned to straighten my back, stick out my chest, and love more. I have a greater love of God and a deeper connection to the positive people around me. I have a greater understanding of why I am here, and a clearer mission for this life of mine. It is not for me. It is for others.

Since asking for one more day, I put a greater value on the simplest of things. Walking. Water. Thank you. All simple, all extremely valuable. Since asking for one more day, I have found out who my biological father is, met my biological family, and been loved by them. I have greater peace, more love, and a path to loving others as I wish to be loved. I have since given two TEDx talks, been a part of two best-selling book compilations, and now this next compilation of love, recovery, and faith. I have also moved to Lincoln, Nebraska, bought a new home, started a new job, and bought a sports radio station in Lincoln with my wife. I have a new sports family to love on and be loved by, and a new nation of rabid Nebraska sports fans to enjoy. And now, I have YOU.

I have a new spine. (Thank you) I have a clean heart. (Thank you) I have filled lungs. (Thank you) I have one more day. (Thank you). First. Last. In between. I am grateful for the angels. I am humbled by the friction. I am elevated by the love.

When facing friction, as we all do or will, I go back to a thing that one of the greatest men I have ever known shared with me.

"When looking to make a decision on which way to go, go forward and up. That's where I will be. That's where everything good is."
-Author Derrick Pearson

Since asking for one more day, there are some things that I carry in my heart with me daily:

-SAY THANK YOU AS SOON AS YOU WAKE UP

-GO FORWARD AND UP
-ACTION IN LOVE
-LOVE IN ACTION
-LOVE OUT LOUD
-LOVE FIRST, LOVE LAST, AND IN IN BETWEEN, LOVE MORE.
-SAY THANK YOU AS YOU REST
-ACHIEVE WELL DONE.
-GO!

ABOUT THE AUTHOR:

Derrick Pearson- Radio Co-Host "The DP and Stephens Show" at 93.7 The Ticket FM Lincoln, Nebraska. Speaker-TEDxLander May 2019. The Love Project. Speaker-TEDxDeerPark March 2020. An American Face

Derrick "DP" Pearson brings his unique brand of energy to The Ticket's midday show, "The DP and Stephens Show." DP has spent stops during his career as a sportscaster, radio and television host, writer, manager, and high school coach. That career has taken him nationwide, including Washington, DC, Charlotte, Los Angeles, Salt Lake City, and Atlanta. In addition to his media and coaching ventures, he also helped establish Fat Guy Charities in Charlotte, an NFL Charity, and developed LovePrints, a national mentor program that promotes Loving and Learning through Sports. DP joins Tom Stephens every weekday from 11:00 am – 2:00 pm.

THE GOOD, THE BAD, AND THE UGLY OF MY RECOVERY STORY
Gloria Mildred Douglas

In the beginning, God created the Heavens and the Earth. What A mighty God we serve! God created Henry and Mildred Douglas who are the parents of Gloria Mildred Douglas. He blessed them with a family of six; four daughters and two sons. My parents both had other siblings, so I also have a lot of cousins—we did a lot of partying! Today, we are a close family.

The good news was that my grandfather, Rev. John Wesley Mason, and First Lady Tiller Covington Mason, Deacon John Douglas, and Lula Douglas were true believers of our Lord and Savior Jesus the Christ. Having the spiritual foundation on both sides of the family was truly a blessing. We needed to attend church, Bible school, Sunday school, youth meetings, and Choir rehearsal. Growing up with my parents, aunts, uncles—all of whom sang, including my grandmother who played the piano—enabled us to enjoy so many good times. As you can imagine, the holidays, cookouts, food, a lot of "fun music" and spirits enhanced everything!

However, I remember at an early age drinking alcohol out of the cups that my kinfolk left on the kitchen table after my parents, aunts, and uncles would leave and go home.

I remember one time when my mother came into the room, she told my father, "That girl's breath smells like liquor!"

I pretended to be asleep but I was high as a kite. Oh, I did get my butt whipped by my daddy. I didn't do that again.

On the weekends was a time when all of us would get together and our parents would party. We would play outside just enjoying one another. I would say, "I'll be glad when I can party and drink and dance have a good time," as I would watch my older sisters and brother and other family members go to Town Hill and Pugh's, and Joes, the Fox Club, and the Hole in The Wall. These were the clubs and hot spots where everyone could party, be hearty, drink, and get merry. And this was every weekend. They would go out and have a good time. And they did some fighting too—but it was only drunken fighting. Somebody would get hit in the head with a bottle, but no one was ever killed. Every now and then, if someone did get shot and die, the whole community would come together and support that family.

Yes, I finally got that opportunity to go to all those places, oh what a good time I had. We'd party hard, drink and smoke weed. We danced all night, (oh what a time)! Experimenting with cocaine was not too popular on the West Side; smoking "Mary Jane" as they would call it, was the drug of choice and alcohol. I was introduced to cocaine by some friends who were very private with it.

We would get together at this certain spot and the owner would tell me to come back in twenty minutes because I'm getting ready to say, "last call for alcohol," and that will be it. He would flick the lights and I would see everyone leaving. I would circle the block a couple of times and then head right back to the club, and it would be On and Popping! I would knock three times and enter the world of Paradise. The cocaine and alcohol were "the thang," and it was referred to as 'the powder that set the club on fire.'

The first time I experienced tooting powder was there at that club a few months earlier.

One of my friends had come down from New York, she said, "Gloria, come to the bathroom with me" and we would go to the bathroom and stand against the door for one another.

This time she asked, "Have you ever tooted powder?" I said, "Girl no, *is* you crazy?"

Well, I guess that night I was crazy.

She said, "Come on, it will make you relax, drink and enjoy yourself with no hangover."

She had a straw that was cut in half, a small mirror, then she took some powder out of the little bag, put the powder on it, took the straw, and put it to my nose.

Then she said, "Inhale slowly and don't blow out, because you will waste this stuff."

I did, and it was a numbing feeling that went all over me—wow!

Then someone started knocking on the door saying, "Hurry up!"

I replied, "Just wait!"

We went back to the bar and sat there, and free drinks were pouring, but it was not the last call for alcohol.

It was "drink baby drink" and dance till the chickens start crowing. That is what happened. The next thing we heard was the chickens beginning to crow, for it was now daybreak and it was Sunday morning, and I had to go home.

As I would leave the club and head to Gaines Street, I realized that I had to face going home to hear my parents say, "Girl you losing your mind staying out all night and dragging your___ in this house full of dope!"

(Back then, our parents called it dope. "You on that dope, it's going to kill you; Fool you going crazy!" The only thing I did was lie down on the bed fully dressed.

My mom would say, "Gloria you are going to kill yourself."

I went to sleep and slept all day, mom had cooked, and I could smell the fried chicken, collard greens, and potato salad. Oh, I was so hungry.

Mom came to the door and said, "Gloria get up and get something to eat, you will feel better."

Thank God for parents who knew how to love their children without being judgmental.

I was ashamed of what I had been doing and was tired of how my life was going drinking partying and getting high. But I was now rested up and ready to start all over again. So I decided to go over to a friend's house, and it was on and popping again. We started out drinking beer and then someone came by with some Mary Jane, some powder—it was not what we needed, but it was what we wanted.

This was another day's journey, and I was glad to feel free and without a worry in the world. However, I wanted to feel numb again and go back to that blank and numb place—with no cares at all. This was the beginning of another roller-coaster ride—my voyage to the bottom of the sea. The current came in and pulled me out to sea and that was the beginning of the storm out in the ocean of my life. The captain of the ship was COCAINE, and his SHIPMATE WAS ALCOHOL. (I put this in caps because it is so important that we make sure to hold to this as our lives depend on recovery). There were times in my life when I used these drugs to hide the depressive state that I was holding on to in the past. Allowing this sickness that hung over my loved ones' lives was an inward, and tumultuous battle. Death also played a part whenever we would watch our loved ones hold on to life for us. Death brought out the tin tubs of beer, wine, and whiskey of all types. I will never forget when one of my uncles went on to be with the Lord. The Undertaker or Funeral Director came by my grandmother's house with this tin tub full of ice and beer and wine. He put it on the back porch. Of course, they said to us children, "Don't you all go back there and mess with this stuff." Well, we didn't, but I guarantee that my other cousins did.

Yes, sickness and death would bring about the sharing and care for family, and sharing a beer or two and a few glasses of wine and gin, vodka, with a little smoke would never hurt. The enjoyment of your family who would come in from out of town would also contribute to this feeling of togetherness. This tradition continues even now, except the new funeral director doesn't supply the booze. The foundation of our family was the Love of Our Lord and Savior Jesus the Christ. This foundation got me to where I am today.

When eleven siblings are living in such a close-knitted family, family unity has a way of always rising. For we were taught to look out for one another. That is what we learned at an early age. I played with my cousins and we would share our secrets. I thank God for the family that I was born into. We all learned life's lessons and could lean and depend on the understanding when we needed that extra help to face whatever crisis that would come our way.

Life will put you in some places that you would never think that you would have to go through. The bad thing about addiction is that life situations can carry you so far out that you do not even realize how you got to that point. One thing to remember though is that regardless of the place that you may be in when you call on the name of Jesus, every knee shall bow.

I always remembered a scripture and a song. For in the time of trouble God will hide you and keep His shelter over you. Thank God for His goodness and mercy that keeps us when we need to be kept. As I look back over my life, I can see how the Lord guided me even when I had done wrong, He never failed me, but God just kept on blessing me. I can recall all the danger that I didn't see or could care less about, that I allowed myself to do because of crack cocaine and alcohol. (I pray that this will help someone who's on skid-row, headed to fall down a slippery slope to hell).

The lifestyle of the crack addict is not necessarily that of the less fortunate. The reason I say that is because the lifestyle that I led smoking crack and drinking alcohol was like being on life support. Your body needs that crack to survive. Each breath that you release from inhaling the smoke that enters your body becomes that high that sends you into orbit like a spaceship. That high is like floating in no gravity. Your mind, body, and soul are floating around in space upside down and turning around with no gravity. The atmosphere is your force. I think about the spaceship taking off whenever the tower is communicating with the astronauts, and then you see all that fire from the ship, as it explodes into the air. That high is just like that experience as I look over my life, I see this as I felt reminiscing over all that poison that I allowed into my system. But thanks be to Jesus Christ, the head of my life.

As God created the moon and the sky, man and all vegetation, these creations exist to help man and not harm him. I then began to realize that the greed of mankind caused him to begin to experiment with the herbs. That's when Satan entered the minds of people, as they discovered how they could get high. The wicked minds' thoughts turned towards making money from the blessing that God has made for man's hand.

This takes us to the poppy seeds in Vietnam. All of the good things created for the healing of the body suddenly turned out to be the very weapon that destroyed the soldiers who were fighting these wars. They brought back contraband with the bodies of dead soldiers to transport drugs into the United States in an undercover way. This was how poppy seed got into America as it devastated the soldiers' and their family's lives. This entered the states and the cities as weapons of warfare for all of God's people to relax and forget about the killing of innocent people and the take-over of oil and weapons of mass destruction! Oh, what a time for the people of God.

So, how do we explain the phrase, "United we stand and divided we fall?"

We fell from grace as the people thought more of money than the effect of what these drugs would have upon people. Memories of all the incidents and all the disasters that we have forgotten about are all in the past.

Now we will focus on the future of our recovery. That simply means that we must trust God and renew our minds, and when we renew our minds, the rest of our bodies will align. And as we align with each part of the body, we begin to adjust to the renewing of our minds that strengthens us through life in Jesus Christ.

The familiar saying, "A mind is a terrible thing to waste," reflects what happens when we take in all that poison and waste into our bodies. The toxins that invade us also fill us with doubt and fear for the enemy is trying to take over. (This is the season when the enemy wants to invade us with his evil toxins and different spirits—as he tries to take us from the purpose God has created us for. The enemy wants to use evil to take control of our mind, body, and soul).

Marijuana's purpose is for the healing of the body, poppy seeds for the pain. However, these substances control the mind and when the mind's controlled by foreign things, it becomes a death trap.

Now let's deal with the addiction. I thank God for the people who were in the life that cared for me, as well as the people who were putting these drugs in our communities.

Earlier, I spoke of a time when cocaine was not a Black person's choice of drugs.

Cocaine was expensive and then some "smart people" decided, "We just need to put this out into the communities so that it will cause the people to smoke it and lose their minds."

We will have the fathers, mothers, sisters, brothers, aunts, uncles, and cousins all getting high. We will also have them selling it and smoking it, then turn them against one another so that they will steal and even kill for this drug. This will inject chaos and confusion into all-Black communities, and they will sling all that dope to their own people. (That is what happened in the late '70s and early '80s in West Southern Pines, NC). Around this town, you could buy crack cocaine and powder on every street corner. The news described it much like driving up to a drive-thru—for they'll serve you on any block.

That is how the West Side of Southern Pines and other cities in Moore County got crack and everything else that anyone wanted. Pugh's Bar and Grill was the hangout spot. Mr. Pugh did not play around with anyone selling drugs on his premises. He would take that black stick and was not afraid to use it. Much of the time they would go on the other side of the street to sell crack. Every now and then you would have a "brave soul" would test their luck and if Mr.

Pugh would catch them, it would not be a pretty picture. He would run them off his property, and sometimes he'd call the police. This went on for years, but the people in the community got tired of all the confusion with crack, drama, and violence associated with its presence. They began to have a series of meetings in churches and at the Douglass Community Center with the Mayor and the police department present.

The community grew tired of the shootings and the loud noise that was happening on the blocks. People would sell drugs, but you would sometimes have those folks selling rocks right off the ground and crushed peppermint candy as crack. I remember one incident that happened as my father was sitting at the kitchen table. You could see down Gaines Street from the kitchen window.

My father said that he saw the guy pull over to pick up drugs, then the car pulled off and the guy continued down the street. Then my father said the next thing he knew was that car was speeding back around the corner. And as the guy turned around, a man ran towards our house. Dad said he saw that the guy in the car had a gun. My mom was cooking, and he told her to duck down because that guy is getting ready to shoot.

Sure enough, he fired off a few rounds at the guy. A bullet hit the brick underneath our kitchen window. The police came, and although the driver missed, he got away, only later to be captured. Someone saw the car, got the license plate number, and reported it to the police. Yes, my father had to go to court as a witness to this. The bullet was also taken from underneath the window. That is how the seniors of West Southern Pines got tired of this lifestyle in their community.

The police began to bust different people. However, as soon as they landed in jail, and the neighborhoods began to get better, another set of people would step up to the plate to sell drugs. As soon as they would get busted, another group would rise to take their place. This cycle went on for quite a while. The law eventually got tired of them going in and out of the system, so more strenuous laws were later passed.

The "drive-thru service" had to shut down, so they began to sell in their houses. This lasted for a while, but neighbors got tired of all the traffic that was running in and out of those houses day in and day out. Generations of families would try to ride their bikes down the streets, but the traffic was so heavy. Again, as neighbors came together for neighborhood watch meetings, the churches also did stand together to help shape our community.

This was the beginning of the war on crack cocaine, better known as the "Rock of Terror" and the "Master of Disaster." This epidemic caused so much pain that I experienced and will never forget where I came from and how I made it over. My soul looks back and wonders how I made it over! One thing for certain and two things for show. God is in the healing business for the prayers of the righteous still avail.

This roller coaster rides the ups and the downs, the fronts and the backs, the ins and the outs. Crack cocaine is a freefall that will land you straight in hell or jail or even dead. I remember so many times when people would do anything to get crack cocaine. They'd steal from grocery stores, and even steal from actual drug dealers! That didn't work out too well for you if you got caught, it was a sad occasion. I never tried because I was too scared to go into the store and steal, but I took a lot of people to the stores to steal. But if they would have gotten caught, I would have been in as much trouble as they would have been. (Lord thank you for being that fence that was all around me that kept me safe!)

I just can't wait to get on that rollercoaster ride again! That was a norm for me at times saying, "I'm through," but ending up on that road of destruction over and over, again and again. What will it take to just leave this destructive lifestyle alone, what will it take?

The ups and the downs, the pains of hearing my parents and my aunts and uncles talk to me saying, "Honey, you got too much going on to end up on this road of destruction."

Lord, it's me again, standing in the need of your grace and mercy. I'm tired of going back and forth with all this mess. I need You to:

Lead me and guide me along the way, for if you lead me, I cannot stray. Lord let me walk each day with you, lead me oh Lord, lead me... ("Lead Me Guide Me." Public Domain).

I remember this song as the saints would sing it at church and revivals. Yes, in those moments I would do great, but then I would fall back into those ways and it would be "on and popping." This cycle needs breaking and I would have to be the one who would break it—I must come to myself and make up my mind to fight this addiction and gain the strength to overcome all the temptations that come with the territory of crack cocaine.

It got to the point where I could smell it in my sleep, even smell it in the shower. Now, that is an addiction! When you go to sleep and dream that you are smoking crack, drinking a Budweiser, or guzzling some wine, one sees that addictions of the mind can get you so bad that the subconscious remembers what you did when you went to sleep. Well, considering all that poison that you just ingested in your system, no wonder you dream about it.

That's some hell to tell anyone—that you can dream about and smell all those demons that are haunting you, to the point they grab you and won't let you go.

The road with the sign that has been knocked down saying, "The road is closed. The point of no return. Bridge out," –all can have you free-falling from a cliff off a mountain with the reckless abandon of drug use.

As the singer Sade sang about no ordinary kind of love—know that any existence with crack cocaine is a love/hate relationship. A voyage to the bottom of the sea with no lifejacket has you lost without a sail. For when you are tired of being tired, you must free your mind and the rest will follow. A wonderfully beautiful change can wash over you—if you allow it!

Let us remember our past and how we went through challenges and changes. From kindergarten to first grade, then developing and maturing from 6th grade to 8th grade, then from becoming a pre-teen to becoming a high school freshman then-sophomore, junior, and finally a senior at graduation, preparing for college. All these different stages of life will challenge us. For our *Wonder Years* can help us as we listen to our parents, pastors, teachers, or community leaders who influence our thoughts and our life patterns.

For me, blessings came with much encouragement from my parents and siblings, cousins, and extended family members who stressed getting a good education and leaving Southern Pines to gain knowledge and another worldview. With a youthful perspective, exploring new concepts, and ideas enabled me to focus on what I wanted to do and accomplish, then and for the future.

Even now, as I am typing this chapter, I realize that I wasted a lot of time doing my own thing. But then I quickly remember that all these experiences helped to make me who I am today. (God, I thank you for allowing me to come through this thing called life; the good, the bad, and the ugly of cocaine and alcohol).

That was when I found myself in a relationship with a man who loved to get high and loved music. One thing that we did well was that we worked and kept a roof over our heads. On Friday nights, it was on, and if our friends (which I had a few in Durham) would come by, we would get high and rock the house. I had left Southern Pines to get away from the cocaine race, hoping to gain knowledge and wisdom from living in a bigger city, only to end up doing the same thing there. Oh, what a disappointment I was to my mother and also to myself.

I realized that this was not going to work. I was just tired of my own exhaustion. So, I decided that it is time for a change.

I was now back to praying and going to church because I needed to talk to someone who I could trust.

The family was saying, "I'm so proud of the change you have made." I told them I still need a lot of prayers.

The situation in Durham was not getting better. I stopped, but he didn't. So, we began to argue. On the weekends I would come home to Southern Pines and visit. He would stay there having a good time.

Until one day, a neighbor said, "They are partying in that apartment when you leave." I told her this is the last weekend this will be going on, and you'd better believe that.

The lease was up for renewal, so instead of signing another lease, I said, "No way!"

The apartment manager told me that I was a nice person and that he had heard what was going on.

He said, "You are always on time with your rent and lately I've heard that when you go out of town, the party begins."

"We are going to tell you that he can't be there."

In two weeks, my lease was up.

A good friend of mine told me of a rooming apartment and the rent was only $75.00 a week, and she said, "Girl go there."

This is another blessing for on that very next day I went over after work and God worked on my behalf. I came to the door and went in, and a young lady asked how she might help me and then inquired about me renting a room. She gave me an application and I filled it out.

She said, "How soon do you need it—two weeks?" She told me as soon as the owner gets in, she would have him call.

"Please get your police report and that will be all you need."

I got home and the roommate was there. We sat down and talked, he told me he was moving in with his brother and wanted me to go with him.

I replied, "No, I'm done with the drugs, tired of all the stuff that's going on and we need time apart."

He agreed and that was great because he left that same weekend. I packed all my things and thank God for having a sister who lived there too, so I stayed with her for a few days. I had some furniture that I couldn't take with me, so I blessed the couple upstairs with it. They were so nice. She shared her coupon savings with me. She brought groceries for a whole month and paid $15.00 for all of her purchases!

The people in the grocery store would say, "Oh no, here she comes!" I didn't get those coupon savings because she didn't work, and she had time, having the other neighbors give her their old newspapers. (This chapter would be the time where God showed his grace and mercy for His child. For when you call on the name of Jesus, and you have a family of prayer warriors, you realize that God is in control of everything and all we have to do is to trust and believe). The prayers of the righteous will avail. There is power in prayer!

In the rooming house, I met a young lady whose mother was a Minister, and she was very spiritual. We would be washing clothes and would always talk about the goodness of Jesus and all that he has done for the both of us.

I began to talk about my addiction and she said, "Girl, God put us in this place for such a time as this."

Work was so busy, and this was that time when it was not hard to get to sleep. My hours were from 7 am until 7 pm. Work and church were the only things I looked forward to. Being at the church was so nice. I enjoyed meeting some others who had substance abuse/misuse issues and we would meet after Bible Study on Wednesday nights. We would also meet on Fridays. This relationship lasted for over four years, and this was exactly what I needed. There was so much that happened, and it would take more than this chapter to tell. God lines people up in places to be there for you and for all who call upon His name.

There were times when it seemed as if it was not working, nights of sweats and nights seeing black lines go across the floor, I'd call on that name of Jesus, that wonderful name while I was hallucinating, hearing from some 1-800 number counselors who would say that I should have had something to help me with the withdrawals. Jesus was who I called on in the time of trouble! God will hide you and keep any harm from coming upon you. All these things are spirits that try to attach themselves to the nerve endings of our bodies causing us to crave that drug as sugar attaches itself to diabetes cravings.

God knows how to put people in those places right when we need them. God helps us through the encouragement and grace of others who have suffered from the same things we are afflicted with. God has allowed me to offer a program at Trinity A.M.E. Zion Church, in Southern Pines North Carolina. This program, birthed in 2017—is known as S.A.M.I. (Substance Abuse and Misuse Initiative). We thank God for Reverend Dr. Paul Greene Murphy for allowing me to tell my vision given to me back in 2009, setting the table for this program's emergence eight years later.

Our mission statement is, "The Grace to Start Over." God will give you the graces to start all over again. You just have to believe that you can do all things through Christ who strengthens you! Just believe and receive God's words. This statement means so much to me—The Grace to Start Over. God gives us Grace and Mercy to start our lives all over again. We can do all things through Christ who strengthens us.

"If I can help somebody as I pass their way, then my living shall not be in vain!" -Gloria Mildred Douglas

God is always in the healing business!

ABOUT THE AUTHOR:

Gloria is the daughter of Henry and Mildred Douglas of Southern Pines, NC. She attended the historic West Southern Pines High School, matriculating from first to seventh grade during segregation, then Southern Pines Middle school in eight-grade, and Pinecrest High School from ninth through twelfth grade. After her graduation, Gloria went to Durham Business College receiving an associate degree in general education. Ms. Douglas later attended Shaw University in Raleigh NC, receiving her BA in Psychology, graduating Suma Cum Laude in 2008.

Minister Douglas currently serves as a local preacher at Trinity A.M.E. Zion Church in Southern Pines, NC. She is also a minister of the Sanford District and oversees the SAMI (Substance Abuse and Misuse Initiative) ministry at Trinity. Gloria is also working on several upcoming books that share the incredible testimony of her life—surviving the journey of drug addiction and substance abuse.

HOW LOUD IS YOUR PAIN?
Hoss Tabrizi

Back in the late 90s brain injuries weren't treated or diagnosed correctly. People would look at a concussion and wouldn't think of it as a big deal.

"Walk it off," "Play through it," "Shoot at the middle basket," or "Be tough," –would be examples of things that I always did.

And now, I'm suffering from the effects some twenty-plus years later.

I don't know if I'll ever fully recover from my brain injuries, but I've learned how to best optimize my condition. Unfortunately, the fear of reoccurrence is similar to surviving cancer since you never know when it will come back.

Brain injury sufferers don't usually get that much empathy from others since people don't fully grasp the situation. There's constant irritability for those with brain injuries. Slamming of a door, dropping metal on anything, a high pitch, multiple sounds at once – all can cause migraines or worse. My ears ring like I was at a concert and they feel full like I was on an airplane. Lights. Oh, man lights are so bad. Anything with a blue hint causes a stabbing pain in the back of my skull. Flickering light or bright light would be the equivalent of waterboarding. Forgetting how to drive home or the inability to complete a sentence because of massive brain fog are some of the minor symptoms. There are a lot more issues that come with traumatic brain injuries, but you know, brain fog!

I want to share a little history about my brain injuries and pass on some breadcrumbs regarding my mindset to help you on your road to recovery.

In 2000, instead of going to the beach week after graduation, my friends and I went to West Virginia. I was trying to impress a girl and flew off a dirt bike at a very fast speed. I couldn't let her know that was the first time I used a throttle. That's not how I operated. Hoss Tabrizi can do anything. A messed-up neck and a bad concussion ensued. My neck and my head still hurt to this day. Older me is judging the crap out of younger me!

In 2004, at the age of twenty-two, I had major back surgery in my lumbar spine. I had over-trained trying to prepare to play college basketball and had two fractures that got much worse because "pain was just weakness leaving the body" and I just trained harder whenever I felt pain. Those fractures got much bigger and the numbness in my leg was much more severe. I had a major dural tear from the surgery and had to be in the hospital for thirteen days.

Fast forward to 2006. My health caused me to fail some classes and take less than a full load. After six years, I finally graduated from college. I planned to enter the world of sports broadcasting. I had a sports television show at George Mason University which provided great opportunities. I was involved with NBC for Mason's Final Four runs that year and did some sideline reporting as well. I applied for positions and got a job at NBC. My dream was within reach.

I was out playing pick-up basketball and took a knee to the face from a seven-foot player. I "walked it off" and "played through the pain." I suffered a major concussion from that incident but didn't know how traumatic of an experience it was. The symptoms from my concussion were intense and long-lasting. I would not be able to look at the lights of a broadcasting camera and complete my sentences. I had been dreaming of being a sportscaster since I was a kid. My mom would videotape me doing commentary with games muted in the background. Dream thwarted. I was not able to work for NBC. These injuries were winning by a lot on the scoreboard.

Breadcrumb Number 1: I regrouped and chose another path. Even though I had always dreamed of being a sportscaster, I didn't let that narrow my future. I became a high school math teacher and a basketball coach. I have loved basketball from a young age, and instead of TV broadcasting, I ventured into the coaching side. During those first few years of teaching, I focused on doing my new job well and being a great coach. I did not pity myself and my situation with what could have been. Instead, I focused on the things I was gaining. In my first year, I met an amazing redhead that was also a first-year math teacher. Fourteen years and three kids later, the scoreboard shows I'm winning.

Teaching and coaching created lots of great experiences that have helped shape who I am today but have also led to a couple of brain injuries. At that point in my life, I hadn't fully recovered from my 2006 concussion and even the smallest bumps, loud noises, or bright lights would exacerbate all my symptoms. Technically not concussions, but the symptoms were intense and challenging to manage. I never knew how long it would take to recover, it could be weeks, or months for the symptoms to subside. Never gone but dull enough to function.

During my time as an educator, there were some sad times as well. I worked hard as a teacher and coach, motivating students and players to work hard and be proud of their accomplishments. I celebrated their wins as if they were my own because I knew that I had helped them achieve. I also felt their losses in a deeply personal way, as if I could have done something to change the outcome. There were six suicides of students in four years from 2010-2014. This was an extremely emotional couple of years. When taking medication for concussion symptoms, you are constantly asked about depression, suicidal thoughts, and if you are seeking professional help.

2015. Wow. What a special year! My firstborn, Maximus, was two and our second child, Mia, was born.

My neck, spine, and brain weren't in a good place from all of my past injuries. It impacted my life as an educator, father, and husband. In January 2015, I had a bad concussion that I got while coaching high school basketball. We were in a smaller gym and one of the players went full speed into me while I was sitting in a chair. I got knocked back into the stands and my head hit the bleachers hard. I instantly knew this was a bad one. I had to power through for the next couple of months. There were important things at work. My wife was seven months pregnant. Plus, the team I coached for was going after back-to-back-to-back regional titles, as well as a state championship. I had to be present even though I could barely get out of bed.

My back surgery in 2004 left me with a numb left leg. Over ten-plus years later year and after much discussion and research with one of the best surgeons in the country and my wife, I decided to have spinal fusion surgery at the L5-S1. In March, I went into the surgery hoping it would fix my leg and alleviate some pain. My leg was no longer numb but due to a complication during the surgery and a difficult recovery, I lost fifty-six pounds. Overall, though the surgery was a success. **Breadcrumb Number 3**: focus on what you gained not what you lost.

In April, my daughter Mia was born. My poor wife took care of herself, our oldest, and our newborn without any help from me. I felt like I let a lot of people down in 2015. I had to take time off from work when I really didn't want to. I oversaw testing for the school I worked at, and I was missing the entire testing season, SATs, AP, and SOLs. I was in charge of organizing thousands of tests specific to students, classes, and graduation requirements.

The school hired a new principal during the week of my surgery. It sounds harsh, but from a liability perspective, the new principal wanted nothing to do with someone in my physical state. When I signed up for surgery, the plan was for me to return in time to run the testing season so that this task would not fall on someone else. I had guaranteed my school, that no matter what, I would be back to take care of testing. The new principal stepped in and said that he would not allow me back due to my physical state. My pride always powered me through whenever my health wouldn't let me but this time, I physically couldn't do it.

My body and ego lay broken before my eyes. Looking at the year as a whole, it may seem like my health won another round, but to me, I took this as an opportunity to turn a hobby into a career. I had been reading books and investing in the stock market for a few years and finally decided to make it official. Another major win for me! A lucrative career that could help support my parents, and my growing family. **Breadcrumb Number 1**: refocus and choose another path.

2017 was another memorable year for me; Maximus was four, Mia was two, Michael was about to enter the world, and I was in my second year as a financial advisor. Starting your own financial planning practice takes time and has lots of ups and downs. The revenue for most in their first couple years in the business isn't the same as an established practice. My brain and back weren't at their worst, but my head game was. Financially, our emergency fund was gone. We had taken high-interest rate loans and had to use money from our retirement accounts just to pay the mortgage. I bet on myself despite so many things telling me to quit. Changing to a career that wasn't paying the bills put a real emotional toll on me and those around me. My career choice was often put into question. My ability to control my thoughts was starting to wane. **Breadcrumb Number 2**: mental health is important.

For my brain, my medications changed a couple of times so I could sleep better to allow my brain to be at its best. Changing medication was never easy for me. I always suffered from nasty side effects. My body already wasn't in a normal state and it didn't like having a variable added. For my brain treatment, there were lots of things parallel to treatment for depression. Medications I took were commonly known in the field as antidepressants—the main course of treatment. However, the prescription functioned to heal my brain by refiring synapses correctly and reducing symptoms. I had to take these medications even though I hated them.

In 2017, I also did TMS therapy. The purpose of the rehabilitation for me was to reset my brain. Transcranial magnetic therapy for most is the use of a magnetic field to stimulate nerve cells in the brain to improve symptoms of depression. With the therapy came constant questionnaires around mental health. I also had to speak to a counselor every two weeks to do the therapy. Again, more seeds went into the nurturing soils of strengthening mental health. Again, **Breadcrumb Number 2**: mental health is important.

Later in 2017, I get a call from a high school friend that someone I went to high school with had killed himself. I was distraught. He left behind two children and a widow. It was tough to see. It also impacted me from a professional level. When I approached him roughly two years before helping him and his family with financial planning, he gave the reflexive response most people give.

He said, "my investments are taken care of, I have life insurance through work, and we already have a plan."

So not only was I not making enough money my skills weren't good enough to help someone I cared about. I felt guilty that his family had to use a GoFundMe. I had now hit rock bottom. Being that this was the ninth suicide of someone I knew, and with all the information out there about brain injuries leading to depression and suicide—I decided to do something I NEVER would have done. Get help and make sure I never commit suicide and leave my own family in shambles. I was very skeptical that therapy would ever help me.

I'm old school. Therapy is for crazy people. Therapy is for weak people. I didn't have any trauma growing up. People in my life loved me. My mental fortitude was something I was always known for. Thank God I started therapy and met Dr. M. He asked to be nameless because he didn't want credit for my recovery. His explanation to me was that my recovery only happened because of me. Well, I'm glad he's not always right. My family is much better off because of him and so is everyone I interact with.

With the guidance of Dr. M, I became a much better husband and father. I used to spank my kids. It was the old-school way of parenting. Not a good tool in the tool belt when combined with a short fuse. Carrot or stick? The stick is often what I got when I didn't succeed in the workplace or on sports teams. But, I learned a child needs love and comfort. Now when my kids are angry and get loud, which may I remind you immediately causes a migraine for me, I ask them if they want a hug. Spanking, yelling, timeouts were not effective. But, a loving reset always works. **Breadcrumb Number 4**: get better every day.

With the short fuse, I make mistakes that I can't control sometimes. The old school way of parenting was the parent is always right. My father was never wrong even though he was wrong a lot. This was a great lesson for me as a father. This information allowed me to say I'm sorry, I was wrong, and follow up with a hug. It's a lot for a kid to think your headaches, your migraines, and your irritability is because of them. The least I could do is to constantly remind them "No no no, Daddy's sick." Hug them and tell them I love them.

In 2017, I also started to learn that my symptoms weren't just from my head. But, that a lot of symptoms originated in my neck. This was a major development for my recovery. I went and saw multiple specialists that could help with vertigo because of it. I traveled hours and hours to see different specialists. Up until this point, if I had gotten even the slightest bump, I could have had concussion symptoms for weeks, if not months. A strong, poorly placed hug would knock me out for weeks and that was just a body blow. I was lucky enough to have my sister-in-law in my life. She's a Doctor of Physical Therapy and is amazing at dry needling. With this new information, I'd go to her and get needled in my neck and the symptoms would last a couple of days instead of weeks and months. What a game-changer! **Breadcrumb Number 5:** surround yourself with good people.

In 2019 my back, my neck, and my head were in a great place. I played a lot of tennis. I swam, ran, and lifted weights regularly. I was able to ignore small bumps that would mess me up for days and weeks. This was the best I felt in a long time.

Everything was moving smoothly until one day while jamming out to some energetic music, I jumped up with joy and exuberance but didn't realize there was a low ceiling. I crushed my neck and indented my skull. I had a massive axial load injury. It crushed my body, my momentum with my recovery, and my spirits. Every time I get a setback it's the same feeling. Why did this have to happen, again?!? How long am I going to be messed up for this time?!? My wife's going to be annoyed with how irritable I'm going to be for days. Someone turn down the volume on my kids and those lights! The symptoms and the pain were really loud this time. My limitations were at an all-time high. Using a computer screen would cause everything to spin. I couldn't see well at all, despite having gotten Lasik years before. The c1-c2 injury made it hard for my two eyes to work together and focus.

Not only did I have blurry vision, but things that moved regardless of the pace would cause symptoms. The symptoms were quite severe. I was fortunate to have met a sweet eye specialist at NYU who gave me a ton of exercises the past couple of years to improve. Dr. K's bedside manner was second to none. She also taught me to slow down, rest, and take care of myself. Something that I don't know how to do as an enneagram type 3.

She'd say, "Use the computer for five minutes, then six minutes, then seven minutes. Use an ice pack. Meditate. Rest. Go slow!"

The use of a computer still bothers me as we enter 2022. But now I have special filters, two special glasses, special drops, wipes, Listerine strips for nausea (it really works!), and other techniques that help me function. Thanks, Dr. K! Since I'm giving shootouts, Dr. Mees deserves one too. He spent a lot of time decompressing my neck. Again, **Breadcrumb Number 5**: surround yourself with good people.

In January 2020, I had sinus surgery to alleviate the pressure in my head and eyes. The everyday use of 24-hour Sudafed wasn't the best idea but was necessary. The sinus surgery was helpful even though I looked like I lost a prizefight. A week later, my wife saw me distraught with a constant flood of tears and hysteria when the helicopter crash that killed Kobe Bryant, his daughter, and seven others happened. My mamba mentality came from Kobe Bryant and his loss shook me to the core. The reason I'm bringing this up is 36 hours later my wife had to come home from work because her heart was racing. She was nauseous and had the sweats. She had her first panic attack and to this day she doesn't know why. I know why. Her invincible superhero got knocked out and it impacted her. Seeing my wife, a mother of three, teacher of the year, wife of the year, and all-around team player breaking down hurt me a lot. The win that came from it was she got into therapy and she started to pick up various techniques that I had learned over the years in therapy. Soon enough she'll even learn to take care of herself first. With everything on her plate and an unhealthy, irritable husband, the Tabrizi family needs her recharged as much as possible.

Breadcrumb Number 2: mental health is important…

Fast forward to the spring of 2020. My Head is slowly improving but my eyes still couldn't handle using a computer screen for more than a couple of minutes. I could play tennis thankfully. But something was always hurt. The main injury that season was my left Achilles. I did about five months of physical therapy to be able to play. Looking back, if I didn't repair my Achilles, I would've ruptured it. I had an amazing physical therapist that uncovered my lower body injuries were from my core and my back. You don't pay the plumber to bang on the pipes you pay him for knowing where to bang. Thanks, Emily and Albert!

The spring of 2020 brought other issues to my head. With the pandemic, our three kids were at home doing online learning. My wife did online teaching of her students and I worked in whatever room was the furthest away from all noise. We were in the middle of construction amongst all this chaos. My brain could hear everything. All the hammering. All the laughter. All the crying. All the screaming. Any loud bang in the house. But, I survived.

Three migraines a day. That's how 2021 started for me. Despite having a history of migraines, it took a couple of months for me to figure out what was going on. My father had survived two months of hospitalization from COVID-19 and a lot is going on in my life. Doctors told me to have my last conversation with my father because he had a 0% chance of survival at that point. It was the biggest motivational speech I'd ever given. With love and divine intervention, thankfully my father survived.

There were lots of scary updates along the way that took a toll on my health. Another thing that didn't help me, though I believed helped my father, is that I fasted for fourteen days. No food or drink from sunrise to sunset. This is an easy feat for most. But, not for those with brain injuries like mine. Even with the risk, it was well worth it! **Breadcrumb Number 3**: focus on what you gained, not what you lost.

All the migraines, irritability, sensitivities to light, noise, and nausea were at their collective worst. Also, the brain and neck injuries regressed because of the stress. Looking at a computer was near impossible. My pain was really loud. I needed an outlet. Somewhere that I could compete and look healthy. Tennis became that outlet for me since I started playing in 2014. During a tennis match, I got a really bad phone call about my dad.

In March 2021, I severely sprained my ankle while playing tennis and had to be in a boot for four weeks. The boot wasn't a big deal. The imbalance destroyed my back and caused me to be in physical therapy for eight-plus months. I would get better and then have a setback. Over and over again. In July 2021, my brain was starting to get to a place that it hadn't been in a while. But then I got COVID-19. The symptoms were really mild during the first two weeks. I didn't even know I had it. We are now vaccinated, but I did lose the sense of smell. However, from week three on, I started to develop a strong brain fog that remains present even while writing this book.

2020 and 2021 took a mental toll on a lot of people. In 2021, five people I knew committed suicide. Their pain was too loud and lots of people around them got hurt because of it. If your pain is too loud, please get help. If the help isn't working, get better help. Embrace hitting rock bottom because it's a great place to be. The only way you can go from there is up!

As you read through this, you're probably looking for the story tale ending that says everything healed and I never have pain during the day.

Even my wife asked, "Aren't you at a low spot with your health right now?"

If I were to focus on all the negative things with my health then yes, my health stinks. That's not how I operate though. It's important to know the progress and the growth you've made during recovery instead of comparing yourself to what it used to be.

I've done a lot of things for my health. A lot. Neurologists, TMS therapy, cranial sacral, acupuncture, physical therapy, chiropractor, dry needling, eye specialists, ear specialists, spine specialists, pain management, HBOT, trigger point injections—all have helped my journey. I've gone to various parts of the country where great people have genuinely tried to help with a master's skillset at what they do. I've seen some not-so-great people that pretend to be experts and were a waste of time.

Am I healed right now? No. The pain is quite loud. I'm reminded of it all the time. People still ask me: How's your back? How's your neck? How's your head? Could I be in a much worse place? Absolutely. Taking a step back and realizing all the things I've accomplished before forty is amazing. I did most of it while being nowhere near full strength. To know my 50% is better than most people's 100% gives me juice. I can easily dwell on the struggles of the last twenty years. But I'd much rather celebrate the wins and have gratitude for everything that I have.

That somewhat long medical history was necessary for you to understand how my mind works. My parents are alive. I have an amazing wife. I have three healthy gifted and loving kids. The business was amazing in 2020 and 2021 despite the pandemic and how much time I spent improving my health. Financially, things are going well thank God. I've grown and learned so much. Every day. I'm so thankful that my brain can still do that. My poor health has made me who I am. I'm resilient. I'm strong. I'm confident. My pain is silent.

Here are some breadcrumbs from my neurologist, my therapist, and myself that may reset the GPS when noise is too loud.

The road to recovery per Brain Injury Medicine Specialist Dr. Gregory O'Shanick is surprisingly straightforward. The four basics of restorative sleep, adequate hydration, daily exercise, and healthy consistent nutrition are critical to have stabilized. We cheat all the time and get away with it in our non-injured brains because of our amazing reserve and adaptability. However, in the face of injury, our brains need managing, in the same manner, we handle our children's delicate developing brains, with attention to these fundamental details, for neuroplasticity to be maximally engaged for recovery.

Another message directly from Dr. O'Shanick when I asked him to advise readers with regards to pain and turning down the volume:

"The event of sustaining a TBI, for many, becomes the reference point from which they view all subsequent changes as the origin. Whether this is accurate or not, one's pre-injury experiences do provide the individual with examples of resilience and overcoming physical, emotional, and cognitive challenges. IF they pause, breathe deeply, center, avoid the grip of panic and then harness those earlier resilient strengths to endure the moment, opportunities for successful mastery abound. Especially for those who have given birth, their capacity to refocus their perspective from the immediate to the goal offers a tremendous advantage in the "top-down" mastery of pain.[1]"

I'm very lucky to have Dr. O'Shanick in my life. He knows so much about brains, psychology, and people. The amount of

---

[1] O'Shanick, Gregory. **10/28/2021**

attention he gives to his patients is admirable. Once again, **Breadcrumb Number 5:** surround yourself with good people.

Dr. M says here are the top four reasons therapy has worked so well for me:

My willingness to be honest.

I go to therapy to get help. I think about what weaknesses I have or what I'd like to improve beforehand, and I don't lie or embellish. Admittedly, I liked to bend the truth a little bit growing up. I'm all about efficiency now. Plus, how can we get to the root of the problem if Dr. M must guess what the actual truth is?

Random luck.

We're a good match for each other. Which is critical in the relationship. We make each other laugh. He makes me cry. Good times!! In all seriousness, it allows me to talk about difficult things and get to the crux of the problem to quickly find the solution since I'm always about efficiency. I was very lucky to have found someone that was a great fit for me on the first try.

Determination.

I'm determined to make a difference in this world. Make a difference with my relationships. Make a difference with my wife and kids. Make a difference with my parents and sister. I'm determined to make a difference with my friends and my clients. Things didn't come naturally at first. A lot of reflexive behavior had to change. I was skeptical that these techniques would work for me and whether I could pull them off. I had to learn to think, feel, or act differently, and sometimes all three at the same time. My determination to not let my health control my behavior towards those I love—had to win out.

Flexibility in my superhero status.

Dr. M calls me a superhero. My health is a mess because of it though. A superhero has a mindset that they can take on any challenge and nothing can stop them. A superhero has invincibility, can dodge bullets, and lift cars with one hand. A superhero has no fear. A superhero by definition helps others, often while sacrificing themselves. A superhero has a moral code that guides them. A superhero can never get injured. A superhero can be in two places at once. A superhero is persistent. A superhero is naturally talented. I haven't fully traded in my cape and tights but you will see me wearing a suit or sweats more often now.

Learning to put up boundaries and worry about myself first is a major change that has led me to the road to recovery. When on a plane or a boat, you always hear put the oxygen mask or vest on yourself first. Our impulses make it hard. But, I know if I'm not here then those around me will have a difficult life.

Dr. M., I can be your hero!

Six things that should help you turn down the pain:

1. **Don't let your pain define you.**

I've had two back surgeries and five other surgeries. I've had 148 physical therapy and chiropractor appointments over the last 30 months. Both of my legs are usually always hurting somewhere whether it's my ankle, Achilles, calf, knee, hamstring, quad, or groin. I get injured all the time playing sports.

People know I'm always injured. I'm usually greeted with, "How's your head?" That's either the easiest question for people to ask or they genuinely care. Doesn't make you any less of a person. You're not the person that had breast cancer twice. You're the person that kicked breast cancer's butt twice. Those scars mean you're battle-tested.

2. **Surround yourself with people that love you and want you to succeed. And make sure to reciprocate.**

What can I say about my wife Carolyn? She's the rock of the family. She is the glue that keeps everything together. Dr. M's voice is usually in my head competing against my instincts. Think of the image of an angelic figure on one shoulder saying the good thing to do and then the image of something devilish nudging you to do the opposite. Well, Dr. M's voice is good and somehow Carolyn usually says the same thing. They sure do love to gang up on me!

Most people look at persons who have disabilities, sickness, or are in recovery—and try to compliment them on their strengths or greatness. When I get a head injury and need complete silence for weeks the attention shouldn't go to just me. This causes twice the work for Carolyn and twice the stress that I'm damaged again. She's the strong one. She's the great one.

When I come home angry just because the grocery store was too loud and it exacerbated my symptoms, Carolyn finds a way to occupy our three kids while making dinner, helping them with their homework, trying to help me—while doing five other things. Most people won't have someone like Carolyn in their life. She's one of a kind, so I'll stop bragging about her. My wife's twin, Laura, has been instrumental in my healing. She has a doctorate in physical therapy and has educated me so much on my body. Because of her, I stopped trying to ignore my pain and learned to use it as a signal to check on my body.

The pain wasn't weakness leaving the body any longer. Seems trivial for most, but learning which alarm needed attention versus which could one I could power through made my injury timeline much shorter. Rest and recovery were new additions to my vocabulary. She spent countless hours working on my back, neck, eyes, head, ears, elbow, calves, hamstrings, hips, wrist, shoulder, Achilles, and adductors. Find people like Laura in your life and make sure they know how much you appreciate them.

You need to surround yourself with other people that care about you and believe in you. People who love you no matter what. Who cares about you regardless of your success? Make sure to surround yourself with people that lead with their hearts.

3. Get rid of negativity.

Simple. Negative thoughts and negative people are not welcome. If a negative thought comes into your head you have to reset.

4. Control the controllable.

Playing sports is my outlet. That's my meditation. That's where I get to be super competitive. Forget contact sports. I stopped that in 2006. In 2021, I couldn't play tennis, lift weights, or go running. I would work hard on rehabilitation but getting healthy enough to play wasn't in my control. Eight months of physical therapy, with skilled and qualified, therapists didn't heal me. I decided I could control my diet and enjoy getting in better shape that way. Not the same endorphin release as exercise but I like to be in control. I had done a bunch of fad diets in the past and had quick, temporary results. This time I chose to use a nutritionist and made a minor tweak or two. I surrounded myself with an expert. We made a plan. The strategy was in place for how many calories to eat and the breakdown of macros. With earnest determination, I planned to be successful and get a little better. Every day. Every week. And twelve weeks later? I was down sixteen pounds. It was in my control. I love winning!

5. Find what recharges you.

What makes you happy? What gives you energy? Just because you took time off from work because you had eight doctor or therapy appointments last week doesn't mean you recharged yourself. Going to the appointments was work. Go for walks. Pray. Meditate. Go get a massage. Use a steam shower or sauna. Write gratitude letters. Exercise. Listen to nostalgic music or bust out some Super Mario Bros. Figure out what recharges you and make it a priority!

6. Celebrate your wins.

Your wins are what give you energy. That energy is what keeps you fighting to get better. Is your glass half empty or half full? My glass is always half full, there is always a win to take away from what most people would label a failure. You must train yourself to narrate your wins no matter how small. I don't count my losses or add up my mistakes, I use them to change my approach, to learn something, to grow, to adapt. Win. Celebrate. Repeat.

Since this book is about recovery, my hope is you learned a thing or two that can turn down your pain and help you live life to the fullest. Our brains are our most important organs. Spend time working on it. Heal it. Rest it. Love it. Feed it positive thoughts only. Since 2017, when I was at rock bottom, medically one could argue that my health has gotten much worse. What has changed is my relationship with my health. There's a picture with two wolves that shows the old me vs the new me. The first image is of the old me—a little wolf with one arrow in its torso. This little wolf is on the ground lifeless. The second image is the new me. He is an older, bigger wolf with roughly twenty arrows in its torso and the wolf is standing strong. The new me wolf is standing with confidence and pride.

The message that accompanies the image is, "life doesn't get any easier, you just get stronger!"

ABOUT THE AUTHOR:

Hoss Tabrizi is the son of Mehdi and Nahid. He's married to Carolyn. He's the father of Maximus, Mia, and Michael. He's the brother to Nahaleh. He's a financial advisor, teacher, coach, public speaker, author, and leader in the community. Hoss genuinely wants to help people become better and discover their greatness within. He cares about seeing improvement in himself and those that he interacts with. Hoss communicates with people in a way that motivates them to have confidence and conviction on their journey of self-improvement personally, professionally, and financially. Just like his father, he wants to leave the world a better place.

REMEMBERING CORDA

In loving memory of Corda McLendon-McCauley, you will always be in my heart, always on my mind. You are gone but not forgotten. I hold with me your smiling face, and your enthusiasm to help others who deal with addictive behaviors. I miss your cheerful disposition. I love and miss you.

ABOUT THE LEAD AUTHOR

Anthony B. McCauley was born and raised in Thomasville, NC. He is the Founder and CEO of MALES (**M**aking **A**chievable **L**ife-**E**nhancing **S**trides) of Distinction/Ladies of MERIT Youth Programs, and owner of Gravity Drone Services. Anthony is a two-time best-selling author, has self-published six inspirational books. He's a life-long Mentor that uses his talents to share his experience, strength, and hope with today's youth. He has completed training at Monmouth University in West Long Branch, NJ as a Drug and Alcohol Treatment Specialist, and also obtained A.A.S in Human Services from Guilford Technical Community College. He is currently a student at Southern New Hampshire University, Manchester, NH obtaining his B.S. in Psychology and received induction into Sigma Alpha Pi (National Society of Leadership) at SNHU. He is passionate about mentorship and life coaching, and education. After attending the Mentoring Center of Ohio, he received career diplomas in the areas of Building Resilience in Youth and treating Trauma with working knowledge on interventions. Anthony motivates and mentors within local school systems and the Moore County community to help students remove hindrances of living life alone. He helps young people make better decisions for their lives and teaches them how to transition from stages of adolescents into adulthood. His motivation and experience lead and guide others on how to grow and strive for excellence, achieve greatness, and speak freely and openly about issues and concerns.

www.ingramcontent.com/pod-product-compliance
Lightning Source LLC
Chambersburg PA
CBHW050333010526
44119CB00004B/133